I Think You Think

30 Discussion Topics for Adults

L G Alexander
R H Kingsbury

Longman

Longman Group Limited
London

Associated companies, branches and representatives
throughout the world

First published *1976
New impression *1977

ISBN 0 582 55510 8

Printed in Hong Kong by
Sheck Wah Tong Printing Press Ltd.

ACKNOWLEDGEMENTS

We are grateful to the following for permission to reproduce copyright photographs:
Associated Press Ltd., for page 19 (bottom); Bahamas Tourist Office for page
13 (bottom-middle); Bermuda News Bureau for page 13 (top middle, top and
bottom right); Beryl Peters for page 41; British Aircraft Corporation for page
49; Camera Press Ltd., for pages 7 and 45; John Hillelson Agency Ltd., for
page 59; John R. Freeman Ltd., for page 29 (top); Keystone Press Agency
Ltd., for pages 13 (left) and 25; Plymouth Public Libraries Local Collection
(Photograph by Reginald Blackett), for page 1 (top); Rijksmuseum, Amsterdam
for page 19 (top); Radio Times Hulton Picture Library for page 31; Syndica-
tion International Ltd., for page 15; The Sunday Times for page 57; Tom
Molland Ltd., for page 1 (bottom); TOPIX (Thompson Newspapers Ltd.) for
page 29 (bottom).

We are also grateful to the following artists and holders of copyright artwork:
David Godfrey for page 3; United Feature Syndicate Inc., © 1970 (Peanuts
cartoon) for page 11; Barclaycard for page 17; John Holder for page 21; Associat-
ed Newspapers Group Ltd., (Fred Basset cartoon) for page 27 top; Modern
English Magazine (cartoon) for page 27 middle; London Express News and
Feature Services (Gambols cartoon) for page 27 bottom; Jules Feiffer © 1972 for
pages 37/38; Money Which? for page 39 middle right; Times Newspapers Ltd.,
(Calman cartoon) for page 40.

Contents

To the Teacher

Basic Aims

The widespread interest in *For and Against* (an oral practice book for use with advanced students of English as a foreign/second language) has led to repeated requests for a similar book at an easier level. *Make your point* was written to meet this demand for teenagers; *I Think You Think* is intended for senior secondary school (17+) and/or adult students. Like its companions, this book has two broad aims: the first is purely linguistic; the second is educational.

At a linguistic level this book sets out to meet the problems posed by the unstructured 'conversation lesson' by providing a flexible programme which the teacher can manipulate according to the needs of his class. *I Think You Think* can be used in a fairly mechanical way for guiding conversation in an unresponsive class, or conversely, it can be used creatively as a source-book for ideas in a highly responsive class.

Over and above this basic linguistic objective, *I Think You Think* is concerned with opinions about moral issues and social values. Most of the topics deal with serious issues, though some are in a lighter vein (e.g. Nos. 4 and 19). They have been selected for their relevance to modern living and they deal with issues which are of concern or interest to adults. The exercises are designed to encourage students to express their own opinions. In the course of discussion it is unlikely that students (or anyone else for that matter) will find the right answers to some of the problems posed, but at least they will be tempted to ask some of the right questions and will certainly be asked to argue the pros and cons of each issue.

Who the book is intended for

This book should be found suitable for:

1 Senior secondary school or adult students at the intermediate level who are preparing for the Cambridge First Certificate in English examination. It may be used in addition to an intermediate course like *New Concept English: Developing Skills* or *Mainline Skills A and B*.

2 Senior secondary school or adult students at the intermediate level who are not preparing for an examination of any kind and who are attending classes mainly to improve their command of spoken English.

3 Schools and institutes where 'wastage' caused by irregular attendance and late starters is a problem.

I Think You Think *has been designed specifically to meet the needs and interests of mature students and will therefore NOT be found suitable for young teenagers.*

A description of the material

Layout

I Think You Think consists of thirty lessons, each of which is laid out on facing pages. A 'text' (the term is used in the broadest possible sense) always appears on the left-hand page while exercises to guide discussion always appear on the right-hand page.

Left-hand Pages: The 'Texts'

Each topic for discussion is first presented through a 'text'. Each text has been kept deliberately short to enable the students to concentrate on conversation rather than comprehension. Every effort has been made to project each topic as vividly as possible, so the style of presentation varies greatly from text to text. For instance, there are four dialogues, two cartoon-strip pages and one purely visual page, and a variety of texts which includes picture stories, fables, letters, an advertisement, a pamphlet, debate notes, etc. Where a particular style recurs, general cover titles are used. So some texts are labelled 'Focus' (i.e. on a problem), '5-Minute Forum' (i.e. general discussion), 'Viewpoint' (i.e. expressing a personal opinion) or 'Well? What would *you* advise? (i.e. expressing personal advice). Most of the 'texts' deal with vital issues and it is hoped that students will feel sufficiently motivated by each topic and the way it is presented to attempt to participate in a discussion.

Right-hand Pages: Guided Discussion

The right-hand pages generally fall into five parts labelled A, B, C, D and E. The five exercises are designed to guide the student from highly controlled discussion (closely based on the text) to the open-ended discussion of topics suggested by the text. Each exercise takes the following form:

A *Comprehension:* This section consists of questions which are designed to ensure that the *meaning* of the text has been fully established in the students' minds. In the early lessons the questions demand straightforward answers: e.g. negative/affirmative tags and responses to Wh-/How questions, some of which can have more than one answer and can be spread round several students. The first five right-hand pages contain examples of most of the different kinds of questions that can be asked, and thus act as a guide to teachers for extending oral comprehension work in the later lessons if necessary. Questions in the later lessons tend to be more interpretative or open-ended. They are concerned with *implied* meaning.

B *Oral Composition:* The purpose of this exercise is to enable students to reproduce an argument they are familiar with and/or to construct an argument of their own with the aid of notes. This section, therefore, usually contains notes from which the students will:

1 reconstruct two sides of an argument (e.g. No. 5), or two or more viewpoints (e.g. No. 8);

2 reconstruct one side and make up the other (e.g. No. 15);

3 construct both sides of an argument (e.g. No. 19).
Occasionally the student is asked to take a stand and state his own case using his own words, or give his own view of a number of solutions offered in the text.

C *What's your opinion?* The rationale behind this section is to involve the student personally either by direct questions about what he or she does, likes, thinks, etc or by direct invitation to comment on the topic.

D *Talking points:* This section is designed to provide opportunity for more extended oral work (e.g. describe or talk about topics related to the text). At this point in the lesson students will participate in free conversation.

E *Conclusion:* This very brief section rounds off each lesson and gives the students something to think about or to do in their own time. The section may contain a quotation or a proverb, an assignment or recommended reading, etc.

Structural Grading

Left-hand pages: The 'texts' have been carefully graded in terms of language content to follow four of the six stages given in the *Handbook to the Longman Structural Readers.* The texts become progressively more difficult, the earliest ones being written within the limitations imposed by Stages 3 and 4 of the Handbook, the final ones going beyond the limitations imposed by Stage 6. However, even though the texts become progressively more demanding, they are always brief enough to ensure rapid presentation in the classroom.

Right-hand pages: Lessons 1–25 are written throughout within the limitations imposed by Stages 5 and 6 of the Handbook, though the early lessons contain fewer difficult structures and lexical items than the later ones. The introduction of a broader range of structural and lexical items on these right-hand pages has been inevitable as open-ended discussion cannot be productively confined to the simpler levels defined by the Handbook. However, teachers should always remain aware of the fact that some of the structures and/or lexical items on these pages will need to be explained during the course of discussion. (All explanations should be brief, not laboured!)

The grading scheme as a whole may be summarised as follows:

Left-hand Pages	Right-hand Pages
Lessons 1– 5: Handbook, Stages 3/4	Lessons 1–25: Handbook,
Lessons 6–10: Handbook, Stage 4	Stages 5/6
Lessons 11–15: Handbook, Stages 4/5	Lessons 26–30: Open
Lessons 16–20: Handbook, Stage 5	
Lessons 21–25: Handbook, Stages 5/6	
Lessons 26–30: Open	

Time Allocation

Assuming a lesson of 50 minutes, the suggested time allocation is as follows:

Phases of the lesson	Approx. time in minutes
Presentation of text	5–15
A Comprehension Questions	5–10
B Oral Composition	5–10
C What's your opinion?	5–10
D Talking points	5–10
E Conclusion	0– 5

The first phase, presentation, is very important since the whole lesson depends on it. A reasonable effort should be made to cover all the remaining phases during the course of a lesson. However, if a lively discussion develops in class after the presentation phase, then the lesson will have achieved its purpose even if the exercises have only been partially covered or—in some instances—completely ignored. It will be found in practice that unresponsive classes will need to go through the exercises systematically while responsive classes will often be able to take short cuts.

How to tackle each phase

Presentation (5–15 minutes)
This will vary according to the type of text. Two forms of presentation are recommended:
1 Listening Comprehension
2 Interpretation
(Note that there is a reference to the type of presentation recommended, 1 or 2, at the top of each right-hand Page.)

1 *Listening Comprehension:* This is recommended for all texts which lend themselves to this form of presentation: i.e. those which can be read through without interruption. These are as follows:

Viewpoint:	Nos. 1, 15, 29
Fable:	Nos. 2, 27
Dialogue:	Nos. 4, 13, 18, 22, 30
Cartoon/Picture Story:	Nos. 6, 11, 19
5-Minute Forum:	Nos. 8, 24
Focus:	Nos. 23, 28
Well? What would you advise?:	No. 3
Other texts:	Nos. 10, 12
Total:	20 Texts

The suggested steps in the presentation are as follows:
a Introductory Commentary (books shut)
b Listening (books shut) (Books open in the case of Cartoons/Picture Stories)
c General Comprehension Questions (books shut)
d Intensive Reading (books open)
e Listening (optional) (books shut)
f Reading Aloud (optional) (books open)

In practice this would work out as follows:
a Introductory Commentary (*books shut*): Say a few words about the subject-matter of the text by way of introduction e.g. by referring to a recent piece of news, thus: 'Did you hear/read about...last week? I'm going to read you a text/letter/dialogue about the same subject...'
b Listening (*books shut*): Read the text to the class straight through without pauses, explanations or gestures. The pupils *listen* only and try to understand as much as they can at first hearing.

c General Comprehension Questions (*books shut*): Ask a few general questions about the main points in the text to find out how much the students have understood at first hearing.

d Intensive Reading (*books open*): Read the text again in small units (e.g. a sentence at a time or less), making sure the students really understand it. Rather than give direct explanations, it is best to try and get as much information as possible from the students themselves, so that they begin to deduce meanings and/or help each other understand the text. Explanations should be given in English, but this should not be carried to absurd lengths. If, despite an explanation, students still fail to understand, then translate briefly and move on.

e Listening (optional) (*books shut*): Read the text straight through again. The students should *listen* only.

f Reading Aloud (optional) (*books open*): Ask a few students to read the text aloud or to take parts in the dialogues and discussions.

At this point students might be given a minute or so to read through the text once more silently to themselves.

2 *Interpretation:* This style of presentation is recommended for all texts which pose problems, require special study, invite personal involvement, etc. These are as follows:

Visual:	No. 9
'Problem texts':	Nos. 5, 7, 21, 26
Well? What would you advise?:	No. 14
Focus:	Nos. 16, 20
Debate:	Nos. 17, 25
Total:	10 Texts

The suggested steps in the presentation are as follows:

a Introductory Commentary (books shut)
b Intensive Reading and Interpretation (books open)

In practice this would work out as follows:

a Introductory Commentary (*books shut*): As above.
b Intensive Reading and Interpretation (*books open*): As above. However, it is not enough merely to communicate the meaning of each text: plenty of guidance should be given to enable the students to *interpret* the text as well, even if the 'text' consists only of notes, as with the Debates, for example. Ask questions to find out whether the students have understood the implied meaning as well as the direct meaning.

Once the presentation phase has been accomplished, the lesson may proceed with reference to the exercises on the right-hand Page.

A *Comprehension Questions (5–10 minutes):* Ask the questions listed in this section (even if similar questions have already been asked during the General Comprehension and Intensive Reading phases). Supply additional questions of your own if you wish to. Try to ensure a rapid *pace*. In the case of unresponsive classes it may be necessary to extend this section considerably by asking all types of questions (e.g. those demanding tag answers). Examples of the range of types of questions that can be asked are to be found on the first five right-hand Pages.

B *Oral Composition (5–10 minutes):* Ask the students to refer to the numbered notes and explain to them any particular difficulties (e.g. new words, abbreviations etc). Then ask two students to reconstruct the arguments or let the whole class join in by referring individual students to the numbered sections.

C *What's your opinion? (5–10 minutes):* Ask the questions listed and ask the students to refer to this section if necessary. This exercise may be conducted round the class or students may be asked to work in pairs: e.g. 'Students 1 and 2' (It should be noted, however, that work in pairs can have the effect of slowing down the pace of the lesson.)

D *Talking Points (5–10 minutes):* When you reach this section, ask the students to read the questions to themselves and give them a couple of minutes to think about the problems posed. Then guide the class into a discussion by asking each question or posing each problem. Students may need prompting by means of additional questions before a proper discussion can develop. If a student makes a mistake while speaking, it is best not to interrupt him. Wait until he has finished, and then point out one or two major errors he might have made.
Some useful phrases for free discussion can be found on page 62.

E *Conclusion (0–5 minutes):* Conclude the lesson briefly by referring to this section, and reminding students of some of the structures and lexical items they have learned. Some of the assignments may be set as homework.

The section entitled *Some useful phrases* (page 62) contains expressions which are often indispensable when conducting a discussion or argument. Students should be encouraged to learn these phrases and to make use of them as often as they can during each lesson.
It cannot be stressed too strongly that the 'set lesson' as outlined above can be abandoned altogether if a lively discussion is generated after the presentation of the text, or by any one of the sections.

Some other possible uses
Though this book is primarily intended for guiding conversation, it may be put to a variety of other uses. Some of the texts may be found suitable for speed-reading or scanning: students may be asked to look rapidly through a text in a limited time to see if they can 'get the point' quickly and accurately. You may occasionally give dictation exercises or ask students to write argumentative compositions as homework following a classroom discussion. Written exercises of this kind may be found useful in consolidating aural/oral work done in the classroom. But it is important not to lose sight of the overall objective of the book as a whole, which is to develop discussion skills by presenting a range of topics which are, for the most part, of universal human interest and concern.

Viewpoint

How many more changes

Sir,

Wherever I look nowadays, there are changes. The other day I went into our nearest big town to do some shopping, and I hardly knew where I was.

There were some lovely old houses near the library six months ago. Where are they now? When did they put up that large block of flats on the corner of the High Street? There used to be a nice little butcher's there—and a good greengrocer's shop. Are they going to pull down the old cinema next?—or move the old church? To me, these are just examples of the changes which are made in our community every day. When is the pace of change going to slow down? When we've no money left? Or when everything we used to know has disappeared?

Things have never changed so often or so fast as they have in the past ten years. It's confusing. It's frightening.

I don't know what young people think, but many pensioners like me are beginning to feel insecure, and people of all ages are feeling the stress of constant change. Everything looks different. Nothing stays the same for very long. What I wonder is this: Are the people who make all these changes aware of the problems they cause? Is the increasing pace of change the cause of some of our social problems and mental illnesses? I'm sure it is!

They say 'A change is as good as a rest'. But let's make changes more slowly and with a little more thought for the effect on people. Otherwise we will have no rest at all!

Yours etc.,
(Mrs) D. Swan

PS I enclose two photos, one of the town centre ten years ago, one as it is today.

Mrs D. Swan

A Comprehension

1 Where does Mrs Swan see changes?
2 When did she go into the town centre? Why?
3 Was she surprised? Why?
4 What used to be near the library?
5 What did they put up on the corner of the High Street?
6 What used to be there?
7 What are these examples of?
8 What questions does Mrs Swan ask?
9 What's confusing and frightening?
10 How are people of her age beginning to feel?
11 What about 'people of all ages'?
12 What does she wonder about the people who make the changes, and about the increasing pace of change?
13 What saying does she quote?
14 Why does she want to see slower changes?

B Too many changes increase the pace of life unnecessarily.
State the arguments

a FOR

1 Some changes are part of life: we adapt to them fairly easily: e.g. changing jobs; moving house, etc.
2 BUT other changes confuse us: e.g. new buildings, new traffic systems in towns: because everything becomes new and unfamiliar.
3 The pace of life increases—many cannot adapt.
4 Result—social problems e.g. violence, and mental illnesses.

b AGAINST

1 We already adapt to changes in life quite easily. Changes in environment for example, create less stress than moving house, etc.
2 Changes are necessary: we can't make progress without them. Towns are not museums.
3 Changes themselves don't increase the pace of life.
4 Also changes add variety and interest to life. We'd be bored if nothing changed.

C What's your opinion? Give reasons

1 Do you agree or disagree with Mrs Swan's viewpoint?
2 How old do you think Mrs Swan is and what sort of a person do you think she might be?
3 Do you think the town centre (in the photos) was better as it was ten years ago or as it is today?
4 Do you agree that 'a change is as good as a rest'? (Give examples.)

D Talking points

1 How many changes have there been in your town in the past year? Talk about some of them and the way they have affected your life.
2 What are some of the changes in modern life a) that you like? Say why. b) that you don't like. Say why.
3 Talk about some of the problems you would be faced with if you suddenly had to live in a foreign country.

E Book titles: Here are four famous book titles: *Brave New World* (Aldous Huxley), *The Age of Anxiety* (W.H. Auden), *Future Shock* (Alvin Toffler) and *Limits to Growth* (Council of Rome). Judging from the titles, what do you think they might be about?

THE STORY OF GLUG
A FABLE

GLUG WAS A
LITTLE MACHINE.

ONCE UPON A TIME HE DUG A LITTLE HOLE AND
WHOOSH! 'WHAT'S THIS?' GLUG SAID. HE SMELT
IT AND IT WAS GOOD. HE TASTED IT AND IT
WAS GOOD. SO HE DRANK IT AND GREW BIGGER.

HE WAS STRONGER NOW SO HE DUG **TWO**
LITTLE HOLES. **WHOOSH! WHOOSH!**
'Mmmm!!' GLUG SAID AS HE DRANK
AND DRANK AND GREW AND GREW.

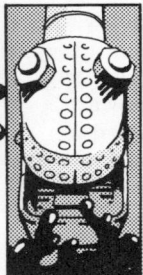

GLUG WAS NOW A BIG MACHINE. AND HE WAS
ALWAYS THIRSTY, VERY THIRSTY. BUT HE WAS
BIG AND **STRONG** SO HE DUG LOTS AND LOTS OF
BIG HOLES. WHOOSH! WHOOOSH!! **WHOOOOSH!!!**

GLUG
DRANK...

AND DRANK...

AND **DRANK** AND HE BECAME BIGGER AND
BIGGER AND **BIGGER** AND THIRSTIER AND
THIRSTIER AND **THIRSTIER** AND STRONGER
AND STRONGER AND **STRONGER!**

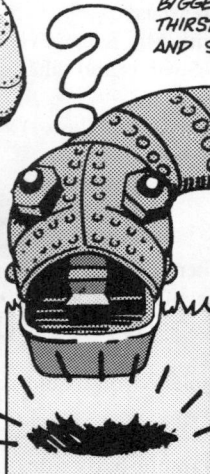

NOW GLUG WAS **GIGANTIC**. HE DUG BIG HOLES ALL OVER
THE LAND AND EVEN UNDER THE SEA AND EVEN UNDER
THE DESERTS AND EVEN UNDER THE ICE. BUT IT WASN'T
WHOOOOSH!!!! ANY MORE. IT WAS JUST WHOOSH.

AND ONE
DAY NOTHING
CAME OUT OF
THE HOLES.

AND GLUG DIED.

A Comprehension

1 What was Glug like at the beginning of the story?

2 How did he first find something to drink?

3 What came out of the hole?

4 Did it smell and taste good?

5 What happened when Glug drank it?

6 What did he do when he was stronger?

7 What happened to Glug when he became bigger and bigger?

8 What did he do when he became gigantic?

9 'It wasn't WHOOOOSH!! any more.' Why not?

10 What happened to Glug in the end?

11 What is the point of this fable?

B Tell the story of Glug. Add a different ending.

a If you think Glug *really* died, explain why: e.g. too greedy; couldn't find anything else to drink; wasted what he found; etc.

b If you think Glug *didn't* die, explain why: e.g. found something else to drink—but what happened then?

C Are these statements True or False? What's your opinion? Give reasons.

1 'We can make our oil last longer by wasting less.'

2 'Oil will become so expensive that private cars will disappear.'

3 'The oil companies are only pretending there is an "energy crisis" because they want to put up the price of oil.'

4 'The oil-producing countries are now using oil (and the price of oil) as a political weapon.'

5 'There's still plenty of oil in the world. We only have to find it.'

D Talking points

Talk about each of the following as alternative sources of energy. Refer to these notes:

1 Nuclear fission (i.e. splitting the atom as in the atomic bomb). Supplies of uranium. Slow reactors and fast reactors. Problem of atomic waste.

2 Nuclear fusion (i.e. joining atoms as in the hydrogen bomb). The way the sun creates its energy. Water as a source of power. Difficult to develop.

3 The sun. Install generator in space to 'beam' energy to earth? Install solar reactors on earth? Great cost—but 'clean' energy.

4 The moon. Harness the tides?

5 Alternative oil sources (e.g. shale in Rocky Mountains; tar sands in Northern Alberta).

6 The earth. Energy beneath the earth's crust in the form of volcanoes, geysers etc (e.g. Italy, New Zealand, Iceland etc).

E Here is an idea for a similar fable: Bear finds big pot of honey—pleased—takes it home— must save it—will last a lifetime—eats it all at once saying 'I must save some' as he does so. Tell the story or write it.

BARBARA GOOD'S PROBLEM PAGE

WHAT CAN WE TELL HER?

Dear Barbara,

When she died a month ago, my mother-in-law had been living with us for seven years. She had become part of the family and we all miss her very much, in particular our young daughter who is seven years old.

Since our daughter's birth, 'Granny' had been a second mother to her. Now she is gone, our daughter is very unsettled, cries a lot and is difficult to deal with. More important, she keeps asking: 'Where's Granny?' or 'Where's Granny gone?' The only answers we have given have been 'She's gone away for a while' or 'She's gone to heaven'. Neither of these satisfy her.

How can we tell a seven-year-old that her grandmother has died and will not be coming back? And if we don't try and explain it to her, what do you suggest?

Mrs D.S. (Liverpool)

If I were you, I think I wo
wait for a

LEFT SCHOOL AND HOME

Dear Barbara,

Our sixteen-year-old son has just left school. He has also just left home.

He is an only child, and my husband and I have always tried to be good parents to him.

The moment he left school, he said he was now an adult. He said he was going to find a flat somewhere, get a job and live his own life.

He has not gone to live with friends or a girl.

But we would like him back home. At least we would like to know where he is. He has not sent us an address or a phone number, and has not contacted us since he left a month ago.

What should we do?

Mrs A.G. (Southampton)

Of course you are worried about
your son, but y   e to

A Comprehension

a The letter from Liverpool

1 Who died a month ago?
2 How long had she been living with the family?
3 Who misses her most?
4 How old is the daughter?
5 How has the girl acted since her grandmother's death?
6 What does she keep asking?
7 What answers have her parents given her?
8 What advice does the woman want from Barbara Good?

b The letter from Southampton

1 How old is the writer's son?
2 Did he leave school and home a long time ago?
3 Has Mrs A.G. any other children?
4 What have she and her husband tried to be?
5 What did their son say the moment he left school?
6 What do the writer and her husband want?
7 What hasn't their son done since he left home?

B Well? What would you advise?

a If you were Barbara, which advice would you give Mrs D.S.? Why?

1 Tell her daughter Granny has gone to live in another town or abroad?
2 Saying nothing for the moment and just wait and see if the girl settles down and forgets it?
3 Try and explain the situation to her daughter in an adult way?
4 Ask another member of the family (an uncle or aunt) to explain it?
5 Something else? What?

b If you were Barbara, which advice would you give Mrs A.G.? Why?

1 Try and make her realise that her son is now old enough to look after himself?
2 Not to worry. Her son will contact them when he feels he has made a clean break to be free?
3 Advise them to go to the police and let them try and find him for them?
4 Ask her son's friends for advice?
5 Something else? What?

C What's your opinion? Give reasons.

1 Do you ever read letters like this in magazines?
2 Would you ever write to a magazine about a problem?
3 Do you find letters like this amusing?
4 'No "problem page" letters are real. They make them all up.' What do you think?
5 'Problem pages in women's magazines fulfil a valuable social function.' Do you agree?

D Talking points

1 Talk about jobs which involve listening to other people's problems and (perhaps) giving advice (e.g. Marriage Guidance or Child Guidance Counsellor, Psychiatrist, etc.). Would you like a job like this? Why/Why not?
2 Discuss some of the main reasons why some teenagers run away from home.

E From a modern song: 'Don't tell me your troubles: I've got troubles of my own.' Is this a common attitude in today's world?

'It's not a hoax'
SAYS 'UFO* PHOTOGRAPHER'

THE MAN who says he took this photograph two nights ago near his home in north London has been accused of a hoax.

As soon as the photo was shown to local airport officials, they immediately said that it must be a fake.

45-year-old Bob Green, who took the photograph, said he saw a large orange light in the sky. He watched it for about 30 seconds, then asked his son to rush indoors and get his camera. When he ~~...~~

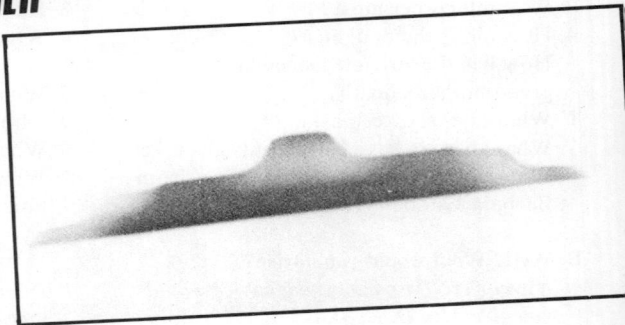

*UFO: Unidentified Flying Object, or flying saucer

Graham has just shown this newspaper article to Robin. They have been talking about it.

ROBIN: The next thing you'll be saying is that there are little green men watching us from the skies.

GRAHAM: Perhaps there are. Who knows? But I'm not saying *that*. All I'm saying is that plenty of people have seen flying saucers.

ROBIN: Flying saucers? Military aircraft, you mean—or clouds, or balloons, or even Venus. Any trick of light in the sky is a 'flying saucer'. People imagine things so easily.

GRAHAM: Flying saucers are a reality.

ROBIN: Then why aren't there more photographs?

GRAHAM: There are plenty of them.

ROBIN: Not nearly enough, and it's so easy to fake photos of things in the sky. And even if flying saucers *do* exist, why don't they land? Why don't the little green men get out of their saucers and say who they are?

GRAHAM: Perhaps the time isn't ready. The earth is still under observation.

ROBIN: If I were a little green man, do you know what I'd think?

GRAHAM: What?

ROBIN: I'd think that cars were living creatures and human beings were robots designed to look after them!

7

A Comprehension

1 What are Robin and Graham talking about?
2 Does Robin believe that 'little green men are watching us from the skies'?
3 Does Graham believe this?
4 According to Graham, have many people seen flying saucers?
5 What explanations does Robin offer for flying saucers?
6 What do people do so easily?
7 Who says flying saucers are a reality?
8 Why aren't photos very good evidence, according to Robin?
9 For a moment, Robin assumes that flying saucers exist. What questions does he ask Graham?
10 What are Graham's answers to the questions?
11 What would Robin think if he were 'a little green man'?

B Two points of view about flying saucers

a State Robin's point of view
1 Doesn't believe they exist.
2 Nobody is watching us.
3 'Flying saucers' are aircraft, balloons, clouds, tricks of light.
4 Not enough photos—many we have are fakes.
5 Why haven't they landed?

b State Graham's point of view
1 Believes they exist.
2 Open-minded about 'little green men'.
3 Plenty of people have seen them—all over the world.
4 Plenty of photos prove they exist.
5 Earth under observation—time not ready for 'observers' to land.

C What's your opinion?

1 Who do you agree with, Robin or Graham? Why?
2 If a friend of yours told you he/she had seen a flying saucer, would you believe him/her? Why/Why not? What questions would you ask him/her?
3 'Thousands of people all over the world and from the past right up to the present have seen flying saucers, so they must exist.' True or false? What do you think?
4 'If a flying saucer ever landed in the centre of a large city—Paris, London, Moscow, Washington—there would be mass panic.' Do you agree? Why/Why not?

D Talking points

1 Talk about other phenomena which many people believe in, but for which we have no real proof e.g. ghosts, evil spirits, the Yeti, etc.
2 Tell us what you would think about earth if you were a creature from outer space looking at it for the first time. What would you think of cities, motorways, canals, atomic explosions, jet aircraft, etc?
3 'People today need to believe in things like flying saucers.' Do *you*? Why/Why not?

E Suggested reading: *The Midwich Cuckoos* by John Wyndham (New Method Supplementary Reader series, Longman)

COURT MARTIAL

Charge Report

Army Form xxx

CHARGE AGAINST
(Number, rank, name, unit
or other description.)

Captain IAN ANDREW EVERYMAN

STATEMENT AND
PARTICULARS OF OFFENCE

*While trying to capture a village on the night of ** April, 19**, Capt. Everyman ordered his men to shoot villagers who were escaping into the forest. Three men, five women and two children were shot dead, and a number of*

Prosecuting Officer's Notes

1 Capt. Everyman is guilty of the murder of innocent people.
2 His orders were: capture the village – NOT murder the villagers.
3 Difference between (a) killing the enemy and (b) killing innocent people.
   (a) is right but (b) is wrong. The Captain knows this difference – has no excuse.
4 This man is evil – murdered innocent people for 'fun'!
5 Must find him Guilty.

Defending Officer's Notes

1 True – Capt. Everyman ordered his men to shoot – but it was not murder.
2 Perhaps the villagers were enemies. The Capt. couldn't be sure.
3 Capt. Everyman and his men are trained to kill. We all know this. How can we try them for killing?
4 Who was guilty? The men under the Captain's command? The Captain himself? The officers above the Capt.? The politicians above the officers? No – society as a whole.
5 The Captain is not evil. He didn't murder innocent people for fun.
   In a war situation, we have to accept the risk that innocent people may suffer.
6 Must find him Not Guilty.

A Comprehension

1 What's this sort of trial called?
2 Who's on trial?
3 What rank is he?
4 What did the Captain order his men to do?
5 What were he and his men trying to capture?
6 How many people were shot dead?
7 According to the Prosecuting Officer, what's the Captain guilty of?
8 What were his orders?
9 Why has the Captain no excuse?
10 What did he do for 'fun'?
11 Does the Defending Officer deny that Captain Everyman ordered his men to shoot?
12 Does he think it was murder?
13 What couldn't the Captain be sure of?
14 What do we all know?
15 What must we accept in war?

B The arguments: make the speech for

a the Prosecution

1 Capt. Everyman—guilty—murder—innocent people
2 orders: capture—not murder
3 difference: kill enemy/innocents—one right—the other wrong
4 Capt. Everyman knows this.
5 man—evil—murdered for 'fun'
6 find him Guilty

b the Defence

1 true—Capt.—shoot—not murder
2 villagers—enemies? Capt. Everyman not sure
3 trained—kill: can't try for this
4 Who—guilty? Men? Captain? Officers? Politicians? NO—society
5 Capt. not evil—didn't murder for fun
6 War situation—accept risk—innocent people suffer
7 find him Not Guilty

C What's your opinion? Give reasons.

1 What's your verdict in this case? Guilty or Not Guilty?
2 If you were the judge in this case, would you (a) punish the Captain severely; (b) punish him lightly; or (c) not punish him at all?
3 Everyone knows the difference between right and wrong. Do you agree?
4 'These men are not evil. Only war is evil.' What do you think?
5 A soldier is ordered to do something bad. He refuses. Is he guilty? If so, what of? And if he obeyed the order, would he be guilty? Why/Why not?

D Talking points

1 Can you name any *real* war criminals? What did they do? What happened to them?
2 If you agreed with the prosecution, then you believe it was right to try these war criminals. Do you still believe this? Why/Why not?
3 If you agreed with the defence, then you believe it was wrong to try these war criminals. Do you still believe this? Why/Why not?
4 Do our ideas of 'right' and 'wrong' depend on the society we live in? Why/Why not?

E A problem: During a war many bad acts are committed. What is a crime and what is not a crime? Make a list of 'crimes' and 'non-crimes'.

PEANUTS featuring "Good ol' Charlie Brown" by Schulz

A Comprehension

1 What has Charlie Brown decided?
2 What has he made a list of?
3 What sort of person is he going to be?
4 Is Lucy going to do the same?
5 How is she going to spend the whole year?
6 What does she mean when she says she's going to 'cry over spilt milk'?

7 What's 'a lot easier'?
8 What happened the last time she tried to improve?
9 What's her motto now?
10 What's she going to regret?
11 Does Charlie understand her?
12 What does he do with his list?

B 'It's too hard to improve'

a I agree

1 Friends and colleagues accept all your habits (good or bad).
2 Part of personality—difficult to change e.g. smoking always difficult to give up.
3 The clothes you wear, your job, home life etc—all formed by events in the past.
4 If you know you can't do better or improve, why try? Accept yourself!

b I disagree

1 May be difficult e.g. to be polite to everyone you meet or work with—but not impossible.
2 Giving up bad habits just needs will-power.
3 Always worth trying—even if you fail; so try and see yourself (and habits) as others see you.
4 You can always do a little better than you think. Accept the struggle!

C What's your opinion?

1 Charlie Brown made a list of resolutions to be 'a better person'. If you were him, would you have shown your list to someone else? Why/Why not?
2 Do you think it's good to decide to be a better person? Why/Why not?
3 What's your opinion of Lucy's decision 'to spend this whole year regretting the past'? Why do you think that?
4 Lucy tried to improve once, but it was 'too hard'. What advice would you give her? Why?

D Talking points

1 At the start of a new year, many people in England make a list of things in their life they are going to correct. We call these 'New Year Resolutions'. Have you ever made a list like this? When? What kinds of things were on the list?
2 People don't always keep to such resolutions. Why?
3 What do *you* do if you try something once and fail? Why?
4 What can we learn from cartoon characters like Charlie and Lucy?

E Two proverbs: 'A stitch in time saves nine.' 'Better late than never.' Explain what they mean and give examples.

14 GLORIOUS DAYS IN THE BAHAMAS

FOR LESS THAN THE PRICE OF A NORMAL AIR FARE !

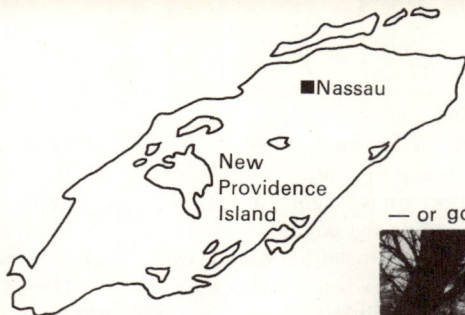

■Nassau

New Providence Island

— or golfing

— or go water-skiing

Lie on the beach all day . . .

— or even skin-divir

Beautiful coral-white beach and clear blue sea . . .

Our unbeatable price includes
- return economy class jet flight from London (Heathrow) to Nassau
- return transportation between Nassau airport and your hotel
- excellent accommodation in one of six

luxury hotels—all rooms have private bath and/or shower and W.C.
- all meals at the hotel of your choice throughout your holiday
- all local taxes, tips and hotel service charges

- the services of one of the company's resident representatives throughout your holiday
- bonus holiday vouchers for sight-seeing tours, self-drive car-hire and hotel extras (see detailed price list)

A Comprehension

1 This is an advertisement for a 'package holiday'. What *is* a package holiday?
2 How long is the holiday for?
3 Why is the holiday (relatively) cheap?
4 What are the beaches like?
5 What about the sea?
6 What sort of flight does the price include?
7 How do you think you get to your hotel? Why do you think that?
8 Where can you stay?
9 Are meals included, or are they extra?
10 Who can you go to if you have any problems while you are there?
11 Are sight-seeing tours, hotel extras etc free? How do you know?

B State the arguments

a A Package Holiday
FOR

1 Good choice of holidays—many different places/countries.
2 Everything arranged—no worries.
3 Sure to meet people.
4 Cheaper than other kinds.
AGAINST
1 Choice limited—crowded resorts.
2 Very little freedom—organised.
3 Meet people you don't like—then can't avoid.
4 No satisfaction planning—just fill in forms and pay.

b A Do-It-Yourself Holiday
FOR

1 The world open to you—choose *exactly* where you want to go—and when.
2 Fun planning and arranging.
3 While on holiday—can change plans.
AGAINST
1 Must worry about detailed arrangements —hotel(s), insurance, etc.
2 More difficult to get information about hotels etc in advance.
3 Can't cater for all family members' interests—causes arguments.
4 Difficult to work out cost.

C What's your opinion? Give reasons.

1 Would this be your 'ideal holiday'? Or would your 'ideal' include other things?
2 Do you like reading holiday brochures which contain advertisements like this?
3 'I'd like to know a lot more before I spent my money on that holiday!' Do you agree with the person who said this? Is there any other information you would like? What?

D Talking points

1 Talk about your last holiday. Did you book it through an agency? Why? Where did you go? When? Who did you go with? For how long? etc.
2 Do you like to have things like holidays arranged for you? Why/Why not?
3 Why do you think package holidays have become so popular? Is this a good or a bad thing, do you think? Why?

E A quotation: 'Now I am in a holiday humour.' (Shakespeare: *As You Like It*, Act IV, Scene 1) Try to describe what 'a holiday humour' is.

8

5-MINUTE FORUM

Crime and Punishment

Situation: *A recent report shows that there has been a serious increase in all kinds of crime in the past five years. But the report also suggests that gaol is not the answer to the problem.*

A group of people have been invited to a TV studio to give their opinions on crime and punishment.

Citizen A: In my view, gaol is a *punishment*, not a rest cure! A criminal must *pay* for his crime. The price he has to pay depends on the size of the crime. For a small crime, a man might have to go to gaol. But for murder, he ought to pay with his life.

Citizen B: I disagree. If a criminal 'pays' for a crime, he can come out of gaol and commit the same crime again. The aim shouldn't be to make criminals 'pay' for crimes, but to correct them so that they don't commit more crimes.

Criminal: We pay for a crime all our lives. *You* try and get a job after you've been in gaol! Society never lets us forget we've been in prison. That's why so many of us go back to crime. You talk about correction', but society has to change its attitudes first.

Prison Officer: At least a criminal can leave gaol when he's done his sentence. *I'm* there for life! I've been in prison now for 26 years. My family and I are cut off from society. Do *you* have any friends who are prison officers?

Policeman: Prisons will always be there—until society finds another way of dealing with criminals.

Citizen C: I think criminals should do something *constructive* and *useful*—like social welfare work.

Social worker: That's fine, but you'll never solve the problem of crime until you deal with the causes—poverty, crowded accommodation, poor schools and broken homes.

A Comprehension

1 According to Citizen A, what is gaol? And what isn't it?
2 In his opinion, what depends on the size of the crime?
3 According to Citizen B, what can a criminal come out and do?
4 What must we try to do?
5 Why, according to the criminal, do many men go back to crime?
6 What does he say society must do?
7 What does the Prison Officer complain about?
8 What does he say about himself and his family?
9 What does the Policeman say about society, prisons and criminals?
10 Citizen C suggests criminals should do something. What?
11 What does the Social Worker say we must deal with first?

B Summarise the viewpoint of each person on the programme, using these notes:

1 Citizen A: Gaol—punishment—not rest cure. Criminal—pay for crime. Price—depends—size: small crime—gaol. Murder—life.
2 Citizen B: Criminal pays—comes out—same crime. Aim—not make criminals pay—but correct—not commit more.
3 Criminal: Pay—all our lives. *You* try—job—after gaol. Society—never—forget—prison. That's why—many—back to crime. You talk—'correction'—but society—change attitudes.
4 Prison Officer: Criminal—leave gaol—done sentence. I—life. 26 years. Family and I—cut off. *You*—friends—prison officers?
5 Policeman: Prisons—always there—until society—way—criminals.
6 Citizen C: Criminals—something constructive—useful: like...
7 Social Worker: Fine—but never solve—crime—until deal with causes; poverty, poor schools, crowded accommodation, etc.

C True or False? What's your opinion? Why?

1 'Prison is a deterrent. If there were no prisons, we'd all be criminals.'
2 'No man is born a criminal. His environment makes him what he is.'
3 'There's more crime in the city than in the country.'
4 'Criminals are ill, not evil, and should be treated like other patients.'
5 'Crime does pay. It's only stupid criminals who get caught.'

D Talking points

1 Which speaker do you agree with most? Why?
2 Do any 'criminals' in this country do social welfare work, or help build roads, etc? If so, is this good? If not, would it be a good idea? Why/Why not?
3 Talk about ways to try and cut down the increase in crime.
4 If you had the power, what would you do for prisoners? Why?

E 'Let the punishment fit the crime.' Make a list of crimes and then write against each the punishment that you think best 'fits' it.

9   Do we *really* need any of these things?

Read
this picture
carefully.

A Comprehension

Study the picture and then answer these questions

1 Have you (or your friends or relatives) got any of the articles in the picture? Which?

2 How long have you had it/them?

3 How often do you use it/them?

4 Would you describe most of the articles as essentials or as luxury articles? Why?

5 Are there any articles which are not luxury articles? Which are they?

6 Why do you say they are not luxury articles?

7 There are things in the picture which many people in some parts of the world have never seen. Name some of them.

8 How long do you think many of the articles will last? Give reasons.

9 How many of the articles are necessary for survival a) in our society; b) in the world?

B State the arguments

a We should try to obtain these things because

1 Many people have more leisure time now: these things (e.g. guitar) help us enjoy our spare time.

2 Many industries are built on producing them: so they help the economy to remain steady.

3 Also many of the articles are an important part of international trade.

b We should not try to obtain these things because

1 Most of them are unnecessary: we *can* do without them.

2 The desire to buy them gives us a materialistic view of life, and we forget about other things/values.

3 They create differences between people, classes and countries, and the 'haves' and 'have-nots'.

C What's your opinion?

1 One family owns all the things in the picture. Is this right? Why/Why not?

2 Imagine that production of articles like these were stopped. What would some of the consequences be? Why?

3 'Luxury labour-saving devices are more valuable than luxury "leisure goods".' Do you agree? Why/Why not?

D Talking points

1 Is it right for people to buy things on instalments that they cannot really afford? Why/Why not?

2 When articles like the ones in the picture are old or have been used, some people throw them away. Talk about other things we could do with them.

3 If you could choose just one of the articles in the picture as a present for your girl/boyfriend, husband or wife, which would you choose? Why?

4 Talk about articles/services which are luxuries today, but which everyone will have in ten or twenty years' time.

E Luxuries: Make a list of articles and services which were considered luxuries a hundred years ago, but which are now considered essential.

One
Man's
Protest

HIS ACTION DAMAGED THIS BEAUTIFUL WORK OF ART

This painting, 'The Love Letter' by the 17th-century Dutch artist Jan Vermeer, is worth over £1 million. On the night of 23rd-24th September, 1971, it was cut out of its frame and stolen from an exhibition of Dutch paintings in Brussels. The painting belonged to the Rijksmuseum in Amsterdam. Ten days later, on 4th October, the thief telephoned the radio and the newspapers and made certain demands as the price for the safe return of the painting. The ransom included:

i) a demand for £1,650,000 for refugees from Bengal where thousands were dying of hunger;

ii) a demand for the Rijksmuseum to finance a campaign against hunger in the world;

iii) a threat to sell the painting to an American if the ransom was not paid.

'The Love Letter' by Vermeer

The ransom was *not* paid. But on 6th October the police found the painting. The following day they arrested a 24-year-old Belgian waiter, Mario Roymans, and charged him with theft, damage to the painting, and attempted extortion.

Roymans' action was a form of protest on behalf of the refugees from Bengal—

But did his protest help them?

People starving in Bangladesh

19

A Comprehension
1 What is the painting called?
2 Who painted it? When?
3 How much is it worth?
4 What happened to it one night in September, 1971?
5 Who did the painting belong to?
6 When did the thief telephone the radio and the newspapers?
7 What did the thief want in exchange for the safe return of the painting?
8 What did the thief say he would do if the ransom was not paid?
9 Was the ransom paid?
10 When did the police find the painting?
11 What was the thief's job?
12 How old was he?
13 What nationality was he?
14 When was he arrested?
15 What did the police charge him with?

B State the arguments for and against this particular protest

a FOR
1 Protest took a new form—made people take notice of refugee problem.
2 Protest was peaceful—no harm to other people.
3 Good idea—could have been effective: people value works of art, therefore likely to pay.

b AGAINST
1 Illegal or criminal acts—rarely effective as forms of protest.
2 Roymans damaged a work of art—irreplaceable.
3 Publicity given more to the painting than to the situation of the refugees.

C What's your opinion?
1 Do you think Roymans was right in what he did? Why/Why not? Can you suggest other forms of protest he might have chosen if he felt so strongly about the refugee situation?
2 Have there been any protests of any kind in your own country in recent months? If so, what happened? What were they/was it for? How effective do you think the protest(s) was/were?
3 What is your personal opinion of people who commit criminal acts (of any kind) as a form of protest?

D Talking points
1 'Protests like this never help the people they are meant to help.' Do you agree? Why/Why not?
2 What sorts of issues (political, social etc) do people protest about? Name as many as you can.
3 'In future history books the 1970's will be known as the Age of Protests and Demonstrations.' Do you agree or disagree? Why?

E A problem: You and your neighbours wish to oppose a plan by the authorities to sell the local park for factory development. How would you protest?

A Comprehension

1 What's the man's job?

2 How does he ask the woman to accompany him? (What are his exact words?)

3 Why does he want her to open her shopping bag?

4 What does she say to this?

5 Does the detective think she has paid for the pullover?

6 The pullover isn't wrapped. How does the woman explain this?

7 Why does the detective ask if she has got a receipt?

8 What's the woman's excuse for not having a receipt?

9 Who's the detective going to have to report the incident to?

10 How do you think the woman feels when he says 'We'll have to prosecute you'?

11 What does the woman offer to do?

12 Why do you think she offers to do that?

B Should the detective report her? State the arguments for and against:

a Yes, because—

1 She's guilty—stole the pullover.

2 She lied.

3 It's part of his job.

4 It'll teach her a lesson.

5 When she says 'Please let me go', she's only trying to make him feel sorry for her.

6 Others will hear/read about the case and won't steal.

b No, because—

1 She's guilty, but admits it.

2 Lied because she was frightened.

3 His job, but shouldn't be too harsh.

4 She's already learnt her lesson.

5 When she says 'Please let me go', she really is sorry for what she has done.

6 If people want to steal, this small case won't stop them.

C What's your opinion?

1 If you were in the detective's position, would you prosecute the woman? Why/Why not?

2 If the woman is prosecuted, she will be (a) less likely to steal again; (b) more likely to steal again. Which do you think: (a) or (b)? Why?

3 Do you know/Have you ever seen anyone who has stolen something from a department store? What's your view of this kind of thing? Do you think shop-lifters should be severely punished? Why/Why not?

D Talking points: True or False? Why?

1 'People who steal from department stores are ill and need treatment.'

2 'If you're going to steal, you might as well steal something really big, not just a pullover.'

3 'It's too easy to steal something from a department store, so people shouldn't be punished if they do.'

4 'It's not the customers who steal in department stores so much as the employees. They're the guilty ones!'

E List: Make a list of measures which can prevent or reduce shop-lifting in department stores —e.g. store detectives, closed-circuit television, etc.

Harry Houdini was one of the most famous magicians and escape artists of all time. He was also well-known for his interest in the idea of life after death. He and his wife, Beatrice, used to do a mind-reading act and they used a secret code. In this code, words stood for letters. For instance, 'pray' stood for 'A'; 'answer' for 'B'; and so on. Here is the code:

1	pray	A	6	speak	G
2	answer	B	7	please	F
3	say	C	8	quickly	H
4	now	D	9	look	I
5	tell	E	10	be quick	J

'K' was 1 & 1 (11: i.e. pray, pray); 'L' was 1 & 2 (12: pray, answer); and so on.

Before his death in 1926, Houdini agreed on a code-word with his wife which only they knew. He said he would try to send this code-word to Beatrice after his death. Mrs Houdini offered $10,000 to anyone who could communicate the code-word. Many people tried but failed, so Mrs Houdini withdrew her offer. Then in 1928 the American medium, Arthur Ford, began to receive messages from Houdini. Over a period of two and a half months he received the following ten words:

ROSABELLE**
ANSWER**TELL**PRAY**
ANSWER**LOOK**TELL**
ANSWER**ANSWER**
TELL

'Rosabelle' was Houdini's name for his wife. The decoded message was:

Answer	B
Tell	E
Pray, answer (1 & 2)	L
Look	I
Tell	E
Answer, answer (2 & 2)	V
Tell	E

'Believe' was the code word Mrs Houdini and her husband had agreed on, and she wrote this letter to prove it:

NEW YORK CITY.
JAN. 9TH, 1929.

REGARDLESS OF ANY STATEMENTS MADE TO THE CONTRARY, I WISH TO DECLARE THAT THE MESSAGE, IN ITS ENTIRETY, AND IN THE AGREED UPON SEQUENCE, GIVEN TO ME BY ARTHUR FORD, IS THE CORRECT MESSAGE PREARRANGED BETWEEN MR. HOUDINI AND MYSELF.

Beatrice Houdini

WITNESSED;
Harry R. Zander.
Minnie Chester
John W. Stafford —.

A Comprehension

1 What was Houdini interested in apart from magic and escapes?
2 How did he and his wife communicate during their mind-reading act?
3 How were numbers over ten formed in the code?
4 So what was the code word for 'N'?
5 What did Houdini want to send his wife after his death?
6 What would this prove, do you think?
7 How long did it take Arthur Ford to receive the ten words?
8 What did 'Rosabelle' stand for?
9 Explain how the code words make up the word 'believe'.
10 Why do you think Houdini and his wife chose the word 'believe'?
11 Why did Mrs Houdini write the letter?

B State the case for and against the existence of ghosts

a FOR

1 A lot of people swear they've seen ghosts— a lot of evidence—the stories can't all be false.
2 All human societies believe in a life after death.
3 All religions accept it.
4 Many things science can't explain.
5 Man has sixth sense—has lost it— telepathy and scientifically-controlled tests prove this.

b AGAINST

1 Mediums are frauds: use tricks.
2 Lots of ghost stories—but no real evidence for or information about life after death.
3 Why should man think life goes on?—if so, then same for other living things— insects etc.
4 Man—superstitious—therefore believes in life after death.
5 Telepathy etc—no proof of ghosts.

C What's your opinion? Give reasons.

1 What's your opinion of the story about Houdini?
2 Do you believe in ghosts?
3 'If you believe in ghosts, you are superstitious.' True or false? Why?
4 Would you like to 'live' after death?
5 Do you think you would be afraid of a ghost if you ever saw one?
6 What's your opinion of mediums and seances? Is your opinion based on personal experience or from your reading?

D Talking points

1 Do you know a good ghost story? Tell us it.
2 What happens to us after death, according to some of the great religions of the world (e.g. Christianity, Mohammedanism, etc)?
3 Why do ghost stories (and stories about the supernatural) fascinate us so much?
4 Suppose you could speak to the ghost of a famous person. Who would you choose? Why? What would you say to him/her?

E Suggested reading: *The Turn of the Screw* by Henry James (Longman Simplified English Series)

TOP SPY ARRESTED

Spy Trial Begins Today

VILLIERS TRIAL:REPORT

VILLIERS TRIAL: LAST DAY

VILLIERS: Jury Deliberates

This is the situation: Egon Villiers is on trial as a traitor. He had a responsible position in his own country and sold secrets to the 'other side'. The members of the jury have heard the prosecution and the defence, and are trying to arrive at a decision.

1ST JURYMAN:	It's no accident the highest punishment in the land is reserved for traitors. Villiers is a traitor. He's guilty and must be punished.
2ND JURYMAN:	Yes, but he's a hero to the other side!
3RD JURYMAN:	Who cares about the other side?
4TH JURYMAN:	Well, I do, for one. It's people like Villiers who save the world from destruction. They exchange secrets, so the balance of power doesn't change too quickly.
5TH JURYMAN:	It's a cheap way of maintaining peace in the world.
6TH JURYMAN:	I've never heard such rubbish! This man has betrayed *our* country! He's betrayed *our* government, and you and me!
7TH JURYMAN:	Nonsense. Governments are hypocritical about spying. Everyone disapproves of it, but everyone does it.
8TH JURYMAN:	Well, if the other side does it—
9TH JURYMAN:	Exactly!
10TH JURYMAN:	We're not here to discuss morality. We're here to decide whether Villiers is guilty or not guilty—and I say he's guilty!
11TH JURYMAN:	We all agree that he's guilty of spying.
12TH JURYMAN:	But we don't all agree that spying itself is wrong!

VILLIERS TRIAL
Verdict

A Comprehension

1 What is Villiers accused of ?
2 Who did he sell secrets to?
3 What have the jury heard ?
4 What are they trying to do now?
5 What's reserved for traitors ?
6 Can Villiers be considered a hero?
   Who by?
7 How can people like Villiers save the
   world from destruction ?

8 Does the 6th juryman agree with
   the 5th?
9 Who has Villiers betrayed?
10 Why are governments hypocritical
   about spying?
11 What is the jury's task ?
12 What do they all agree ?
13 What don't they agree about?
14 What do you think they recommended ?

B 'Spying is wrong.' Do you agree or disagree?

a YES, spying is wrong

1 Spies betray own country—government—
   own families—for money.
2 Spies use people—always wrong.
3 Spies take away from own country any
   advantage (in balance of power) from
   new discoveries etc.
4 They therefore deserve the most severe
   punishment—death.

b NO, spying isn't wrong

1 Spies exchange secret information—
   keep world balance of power—maintain
   peace.
2 All governments hypocrites—all employ
   spies—recognised—all do it.
3 Spies should be world heroes: Don't
   punish them! Reward them!

C What's your opinion? Give reasons.

1 Which juryman/jurymen do you agree with most?
2 What, in your opinion, *is* spying?
3 Do stories about spies give us a true picture, do you think?
4 What qualities do you think a man (or woman) needs to become a spy? What do you base
   your opinion on?
5 Do you think it's wrong to spy?
6 If you think it's wrong, do you think it's wrong for your country to employ spies?
7 If you think it's right, would *you* spy?
8 Are governments really hypocritical about spying?

D Talking points

1 How would you feel if a friend gave away your secrets? Is spying the same?
2 Should a spy be punished? If not, why not? If so, how?
3 What's the highest form of punishment in this country? Who is it reserved for? Is it common? Why/Why not?
4 Do you know of any important spy cases? Tell us about them/one.
5 What do you understand by the 'balance of power'?
6 Talk about spying methods.

E Suggested reading: *The Thirty-Nine Steps* by John Buchan (Longman Simplified English
   Series)

1

2

3

A Comprehension

Look at the first cartoon

1 Where has the woman been?
2 What does she shout when she comes in?
3 What did she win? What for?
4 Is her husband very interested? How do you know?
5 What happened when *he* won it?

Look at the second cartoon

6 How does the woman describe her son?
7 What's he doing to his mother (according to her)?

8 What does she swear? What does it mean, do you think?
9 What does the boy offer to do?
10 Does his mother want him to do that? Why not?

Look at the third cartoon

11 Does the woman look very happy in the first picture? Why not? (Describe the state of the room.)
12 What does she do?
13 What has her husband been doing?
14 Why is the woman crying in the last picture?

B Well? What would you advise?

1 Study each cartoon again. Say what (might have) happened *before* this scene; what is happening now; and what you think could happen next.
2 For each cartoon, say a) what you would advise *him* to do/not to do.
                             b) what you would advise *her* to do/not to do.
For each piece of advice you give, also give a reason or reasons.

C What's your opinion?

1 'In order to enjoy these English cartoons, you must be English yourself.' Do you agree? Why/Why not?
2 How would you feel if you were the woman in each cartoon? Why? Would you have reacted in the same way, do you think?
3 How would you react if you were the man/boy in each cartoon? Why? Or perhaps you would never get into any of the situations. True or not?
4 Do you find these cartoons amusing? Can you say why/why not? Can you also say if one strikes you as a) particularly amusing; or b) not at all funny? Why?

D Talking points

1 Talk about other people's personal habits which annoy you (e.g. reading the paper when you're talking to them; making a mess of a clean room; not putting things away where they found them; etc). Do you try to live with such habits (Why?) or do you try and 'correct' them (Why and how?)?
2 Talk about strip cartoons which you read regularly. What can you say about the characters? Why do you enjoy reading the cartoons? Why do you think they are generally popular?
3 Can you name any other cartoons in which animals play an important role (as in the Fred Basset cartoon)? Why do you think cartoonists often put words into the mouths of animals?

E Assignment: Choose a political or 'domestic' cartoon from one of today's newspapers. What message is it trying to convey?

Viewpoint

Cars on a scrap heap

Mr R. Philpott

Waste not, want not!

Sir,

Once upon a time (and not very long ago, either!) industrial goods were made to last for ever. If you bought a car or a cooker, it was a once-in-a-lifetime investment. You paid good money for the article and you looked after it. Nowadays industry has persuaded us that its products can only last a very short time. It's cheaper to throw them away than to repair them. This has led directly to the 'throw-away society' and to the waste of the earth's resources. Just think of the cars that are traded in daily simply because they are 'out of fashion'. Just think of the expensive packaging material that is thrown away each time a new object is bought—material which we the consumers must pay for! Our industrial society has turned us into spoilt children. It's this terrible wastefulness that has got us into the mess we are in now. When there are no resources left, we'll start to look after what we have. But why can't we act *before* this happens? Why can't we go back to a society in which the prevention of waste is a virtue?

Yours etc.,

(Mr) R. Philpott

'Friends of the Earth' returning 'non-returnable' bottles to a soft drink factory

A Comprehension

1 How well were industrial goods made once? How long ago?
2 What sort of investment did a car or a cooker use to be? Why?
3 What has industry done to us?
4 Why don't we repair many things?
5 What has this attitude led to?
6 Why are many cars traded in?
7 What is thrown away when we buy a new article? Who pays for it?
8 What has turned us into 'spoilt children'?
9 According to Mr Philpott, when will we start to look after what we have?
10 What sort of society does Mr Philpott want to see?

B Waste not, want not!

a State Mr Philpott's argument

1 Not long ago—goods made to last. Large article—lifetime investment. Paid—looked after it.
2 Now—cheaper to throw away than repair: 'throw-away society'.
3 Wrapping and packaging—a waste.
4 Result of wastefulness—shortage of world's resources. These are permanent e.g. steel, oil, paper.
5 Solutions: waste less; make more things to last; recycle waste.

b Construct a counter-argument

1 Society not built now on permanence.
2 People want greater variety of goods—well and attractively packaged.
3 Manufacturers provide what public wants: changing tastes and fashions.
4 People move around more than in the past—don't want or need to acquire as many large permanent possessions.
5 Industry couldn't afford to produce articles to last a lifetime: production based on constant demand. Employment for thousands.

C What's your opinion?

1 Do you agree with Mr Philpott that we should 'go back to a society in which prevention of waste is a virtue'? Why/Why not?
2 Which would you rather do: buy a cheap car which you can afford now, or save up for a very good car which will last a long time? Why?
3 'Advertisers are mainly to blame for the throw-away society.' What do you think? Why?

D Talking points

1 Talk about the different things you buy from day to day. Which have more wrapping or packaging than they need, or are described as 'non-returnable' or 'disposable'. Make a list.
2 'No one has begun to tackle the problem of waste seriously.' What do you think? If you were given the power to try and solve the waste problem in this country, what are some of the laws you would make? Give your reasons.
3 Prevention of waste was only one of our grandparents' virtues. What others can you think of that we seem to have lost or forgotten?

E Proverbs: Discuss the old-fashioned virtues implied in these proverbs: '*Enough is as good as a feast.*' '*Look after the pennies, and the pounds will look after themselves.*' '*Waste not, want not.*'

FOCUS ON ASTROLOGY

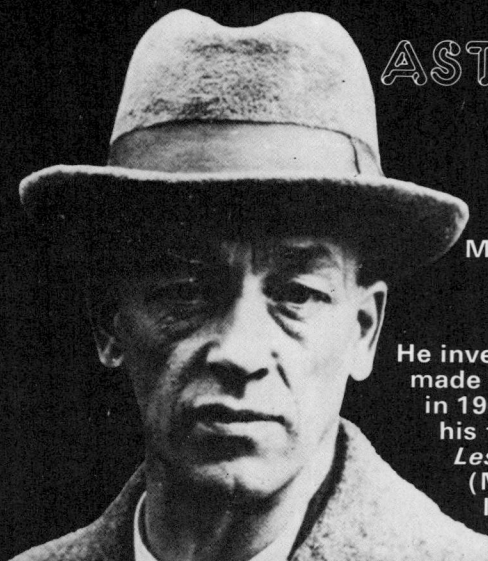

M. Michel Gauquelin
is a graduate
of the Sorbonne
in statistics.
He investigated the claims
made by astrologers and
in 1960 published a book about
his findings called
Les Hommes et les Astres
(Man and the Stars).
In this book M. Gauquelin
shows that there is a
relationship between the
position of the planets at
the moment people are born
and their choice of
profession. M. Gauquelin
collected information about
more than 25,000 people from
different countries.

Here are some of his
statistical results:

James Stephens and James Joyce, Irish writers,
both born 6.00 a.m., 2 February 1882

Beniamino Gigli and Lauritz Melchior,
tenors, both born 20 March 1890

Nobel Prize-winners Albert Einstein
and Otto Hahn, both born 14 March 1879

Rising and setting of	Significant frequency	Average frequency	Significantly low frequency
MARS	Scientists Doctors Athletes Executives	Politicians Actors Journalists	Writers Painters Musicians
JUPITER	Team athletes Soldiers Politicians Actors Journalists Playwrights	Painters Musicians Writers	Solo athletes (boxers, etc) Scientists Doctors
SATURN	Scientists Doctors	Politicians Soldiers	Actors Painters Journalists Writers
MOON	Politicians Writers	Scientists Doctors Painters Musicians Journalists	Athletes Soldiers

A Comprehension

1 What does M. Gauquelin show in his book *Man and the Stars*?
2 How much information did M. Gauquelin base his findings on?
3 Judging from the distribution of professions in the table, what qualities would you associate with Mars, Jupiter, Saturn and the Moon?
4 Why do you think there is a difference between 'writers', 'journalists' and 'playwrights'? Do you think there should be? Why?
5 What interesting fact can you discover about politicians?
6 A friend of yours is a journalist who wants to change his profession. What new profession would you advise for him, according to the table? Why?
7 What conclusions can you draw about introvert and extrovert personalities?

B State the case for and against astrology:

a FOR

1 Very ancient practice—still grips men's imagination—worldwide.
2 It is a serious 'science'—don't judge it from newspaper horoscopes.
3 Plenty of evidence—e.g. lives of famous people, statistics, etc.
4 Even scientists agree—many things in universe we don't understand.
5 Scientists say—many things influence us— why not the stars?
6 Critics should really study the evidence: they're too prejudiced.

b AGAINST

1 Unscientific rubbish—began *before* we knew about the solar system.
2 New planets found in recent times—so 'planetary influence' nonsense.
3 How can anything 'influence' us at such great distances?
4 How can lifeless matter (i.e. planets) affect living things?
5 Scientifically, we inherit our characteristics from our parents.
6 Statements made by astrologers are too vague—many interpretations.

C What's your opinion?

1 Do you believe in astrology? Why/Why not?
2 Do you read your horoscope every day? Why/Why not?
3 What did your horoscope say about yesterday? Did it happen? What does this prove?
4 If you believe in astrology, then you believe we have no control over our lives. Do you agree with this statement?
5 If you don't believe in astrology, then you believe we can shape our own lives. Do you agree with this statement?

D Talking points

1 Talk about the characteristics of people born under Leo, Aquarius, Taurus etc.
2 Is it good or bad to know about the future? Why?
3 If you compare the forecasts made on the horoscope page in six different papers in any one day, they will not be the same. Why?

E Assignment: Find out about the six men in the photos. Report on any two of them.

The arguments FOR 'People are Pollution'

1 Pollution is increasing. People create pollution. Therefore if we want less pollution, we must have fewer people.

2 We destroy living things for the benefit of people, but people cannot exist without living things,— therefore we must have fewer people.

3 There is only a limited amount of land. As the population grows, we have to farm more land for food and build more houses : in this way we destroy the land and there will be famines.

4 Solution : the government must have a population policy : e.g. 'It's against the law to have more than two children' or : 'If you have more than two children, you will have to pay more tax.'

---

1 Those who want fewer people hate mankind. People are *not* less important than (say) trees. (Are YOU ?)

2 Who can really say that there are too many people in the world ?

3 It is only cities that are overcrowded— not the whole world.

There would not be less 'pollution' with fewer people : there would probably be just as much—from industry, cities, the motor car etc.

5 If we had fewer people, then think of the effects on (a) industry (—it would suffer—) ; and on (b) society (—there would be more old people than young—).

6 A population policy is politically unacceptable.

During the course of this debate, about 7,000 children will be born into the world. About 3,000 people will die. This gap will add 65 million people to the world population in the next 12 months.

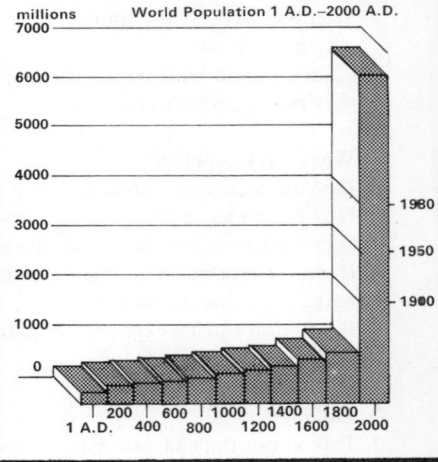

millions — World Population 1 A.D.–2000 A.D.

7000
6000
5000
4000
3000 — 1980
2000 — 1950
1000 — 1900
0

1 A.D. 200 400 600 800 1000 1200 1400 1600 1800 2000

The arguments AGAINST

A Comprehension
1 What will happen to the world population in the next 12 months?
2 Why must we have fewer people?
3 Why do we destroy living things?
4 Why will there be famines if there are more people?
5 What is meant by a 'population policy'?
6 Who hates mankind?
7 Is the whole world overcrowded?
8 Would fewer people mean less pollution?
9 What effects would a small population have on (a) industry, and (b) society?

B Refer to these notes and conduct the debate:
a FOR
1 Pollution—increasing. People create pollution. If—less pollution—fewer people.
2 Destroy living things—people—but can't exist—therefore fewer.
3 Limited land—population grows—farm—houses—famines.
4 Solution—population policy—two children—more than two—tax.

b AGAINST
1 Hate mankind—people—trees.
2 Who can really say—too many people?
3 Cities overcrowded—not world.
4 Not less pollution if fewer people—probably just as much.
5 If fewer people, then—effects on (a) industry, and (b) society.
6 Policy—politically unacceptable.

Add other points made by the class

C What's your opinion? Give reasons.
1 Which of the two arguments do you agree with?
2 Would a population policy work in this country?
3 Would this country suffer or benefit if there were more people?
4 'Population is the least of our problems nowadays.' What do you think?
5 What is an acceptable standard of living?
6 What is being done to house people in this country? Is it enough, do you think? Or could more be done? What, for example?

D Talking points
1 Is birth control right or wrong? Why?
2 What are your views on (a) emigration and (b) immigration?
3 Talk about the world population. Which parts of the world are overcrowded? Why? Which parts are underpopulated? Why? What could we learn from this?
4 Talk about the effects of an increase in the population of a village on resources e.g. water supplies, schools, roads, housing, hospitals etc.

E Opinion:
Here is a 19th century opinion by Thomas Malthus. Do you think it is an inhuman statement? Why/Why not?
'. . .if he cannot get subsistence from his parents on whom he has a just demand, and if society does not want his labour, (he) has no claim of *right* to the smallest portion of food and in fact has no right to be where he is.'

18   Life begins at 40

An argument between Daphne (aged 20) and Robin (aged 40).

DAPHNE: Are you seriously trying to argue that life begins at 40? Life begins nine months before birth! And what do you mean by 'life begins' anyway?

ROBIN: Well, I don't mean life begins at 40 in a literal sense, of course. But I do mean a number of things. Here are some of them. Assuming your health is good, at the age of 40
you are still young enough to enjoy yourself;
you can afford to enjoy yourself;
you are mature and experienced, so you can assess
     situations and deal with them;
you can deal with the opposite sex with skill;
you can enjoy some of the fruits of your efforts—in
     the family, at home and at work;
you are at the height of your mental powers;
you can see clearly the direction your life is taking;
—*and* you have a settled existence.

DAPHNE: What about the other side of things?
You've lost most of your youthful vigour and energy;
life lacks excitement because you are so settled that you can
     almost predict what every day is going to bring;
you've become bourgeois and conservative;
you're putting on weight, losing your hair, going grey, or
     your eyesight is beginning to fail;
you're worried *because* you've got possessions and responsibilities. The best
     is over for you;
       it's too late to do anything about your life if you've
         made a mess of it. It can't be undone!
         And what have you got to look forward to?
         Just old age.

A Comprehension

1 Who's arguing that life begins at 40? Why?
2 What does Robin mean by 'I don't mean...in a literal sense'?
3 According to Robin, if you want to enjoy yourself, you need two things. What are they?
4 In his opinion, what do you need in order to assess a situation and deal with it?

5 What are some of the other things you can enjoy at 40?
6 According to Daphne, why does life for a 40-year-old lack excitement?
7 What, in her opinion, is happening physically to a 40-year-old?
8 Why, in her opinion, is a 40-year-old likely to worry?
9 If you've made a mess of your life, what can't you do at the age of 40?

B Two points of view about 40-year-olds

a State Robin's point of view
1 young enough—enjoy themselves.
2 can afford—enjoy themselves.
3 mature—assess/deal with situations.
4 deal with opposite sex.
5 enjoy—efforts—family etc.
6 height—mental powers.
7 see clearly—direction—life.
8 settled existence.

b State Daphne's point of view
1 lost vigour—energy.
2 life—no excitement—predict every day.
3 bourgeois—conservative.
4 weight—hair—grey—eyesight.
5 worried—possessions, etc.
6 best—over—too late—mess.
7 look forward to?—old age.

C What's your opinion?

Robin assumes that young people: are poor, immature, inexperienced; can't assess situations and deal with them; can't get on with the opposite sex; haven't created their own families or homes; haven't made progress in their work/career; can't see what direction their life is taking; don't have a settled existence.

Daphne assumes that middle-aged people: aren't energetic; lead unexciting lives; are conservative; are already showing signs of old age; have possessions and responsibilities; are past their best; and only have old age to look forward to.

1 Do you agree with these assumptions? Why/Why not?
2 Could Robin's assumptions apply to 40-year-olds? In what circumstances?
3 Could Daphne's assumptions apply to 20-year-olds? In what circumstances?

D Talking points

1 If you're under 40, what is your view of 40-year-olds today?
2 If you're over 40, what is your view of 20-year-olds today?
3 'You're as old as you feel.' Would you agree? Why/Why not?

E A quotation: 'Grow old along with me, the best is yet to be.' (Robert Browning). What do you think 'old' means to 10, 20, 30, 40 and 50-year-olds?

I DON'T KNOW WHAT TO DO ABOUT IT—

BUT MY TELEPHONE IS GROWING.

I DON'T WATER IT—OR FEED IT—OR KEEP IT IN THE SUN—

BUT EVERY TIME IT RINGS IT GETS BIGGER.

AND I WISH THEY'D TAKE IT OUT

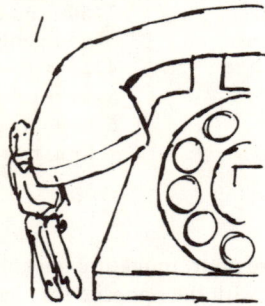

BUT THEY TOLD ME THERE'S A WAITING LIST TO HAVE YOUR PHONE TAKEN OUT.

*The telephone repair people

A Comprehension

1 What is the man worried about?
2 Does he know what to do?
3 What doesn't he do to his telephone?
4 When does it get bigger?
5 Who took a look at it?
6 What did they say?

7 What does it interfere with?
8 Why does the man wish the telephone people would take it out?
9 Why can't they take it out now?
10 When will they call again? Why?
11 What has happened to the man in the last picture?

B Is the telephone a blessing or a curse? State the arguments

a *It's a blessing because it*

1 helps us communicate more easily—thus extension of voice and ear.
2 is invaluable in emergencies (e.g. fire, police, ambulance etc).
3 provides direct link between world leaders (e.g. White House-Kremlin 'hot line')—world peace.
4 allows quick decisions to be conveyed (e.g. in industry)—thus saves time—distance not important.

b *It's a curse because it*

1 intrudes on our privacy.
2 makes us dependent on it—and perhaps lazy e.g. we stop writing letters.
3 can be used by anyone for a joke e.g. wrong numbers and anonymous calls etc.
4 can be used by secret services or criminals to obtain information e.g. by phone-tapping.

TELEPHONE REPAIR* TOOK A LOOK AT IT—

BUT THEY SAID THEY DIDN'T SEE ANYTHING WRONG WITH IT.

BUT IT INTERFERES WITH MY INDEPENDENCE,

AND THEY'D CALL ME IN SIX MONTHS TO SEE IF I HAVEN'T CHANGED MY—

BZZZZZZZ

C What's your opinion?

1 Do you think this cartoon is just about a telephone that grows bigger, or something else? Why do you think that?

2 Do the telephone, gas, electricity and water companies in this country provide good services? Could they be improved? How?

3 Are you on a waiting list for anything at the moment? Have you ever been in the past? What for? Do you like waiting lists? Why/Why not?

4 What's your opinion of 'answer-phones'?

D Talking points

1 Have you got a telephone at home? If so, how often does it ring in a day?

2 Have you got a telephone at work? Is it essential?—or could you do without it? Do you ring out much, or do other people ring you? Why?

3 Would you like to be without a telephone—at home or at work? Why/Why not?

4 Talk about some occasions when a) the telephone has been a blessing to you; and b) when it has been a terrible nuisance.

5 Do you think people in the past were happier without things like the telephone, radio, television, etc? Why/Why not?

E Television—a blessing or a curse?
Write a list of advantages and disadvantages of the television—rather like the arguments for and against the telephone.

38

20 We all suffer from inflation. We all agree that it's a bad thing. The bread-winner's pay-packet gets smaller and smaller. The housewife can hardly keep up with the rising cost of living because the housekeeping money buys less and less. People on fixed incomes (e.g. pensioners) suffer particularly. Who can—or even wants to—save money when prices are going up and up and up?

So what can be done to control inflation? Consider these proposals:

The Government should
- not print more money.
- cut its own spending.
- raise taxes.
- ban all hire purchase agreements.
- create unemployment.
- control wages and prices.
- control company profits.
- bring down interest rates
- introduce a system of 'indexing'.*

These measures might cure inflation, but are they worse than the evil we wish to cure? That's the question.

THE RATE OF INFLATION THROUGHOUT THE WORLD (1974)

FOCUS ON INFLATION

CONSUMER PIE (Great Britain)
The size of a slice shows the relative importance given to that particular group of things at the start of 1974.

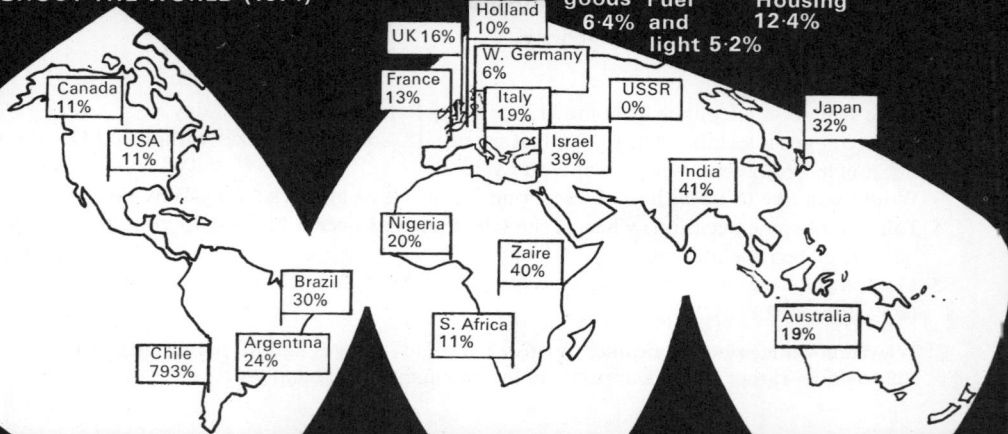

- Eating out 1%
- Services 5·4%
- Food 25·3%
- Miscellaneous 6·3%
- Alcohol 7%
- Tobacco 4·3%
- Transport and vehicles 13·5%
- Clothing 9·1%
- Household goods 6·4%
- Fuel and light 5·2%
- Housing 12·4%

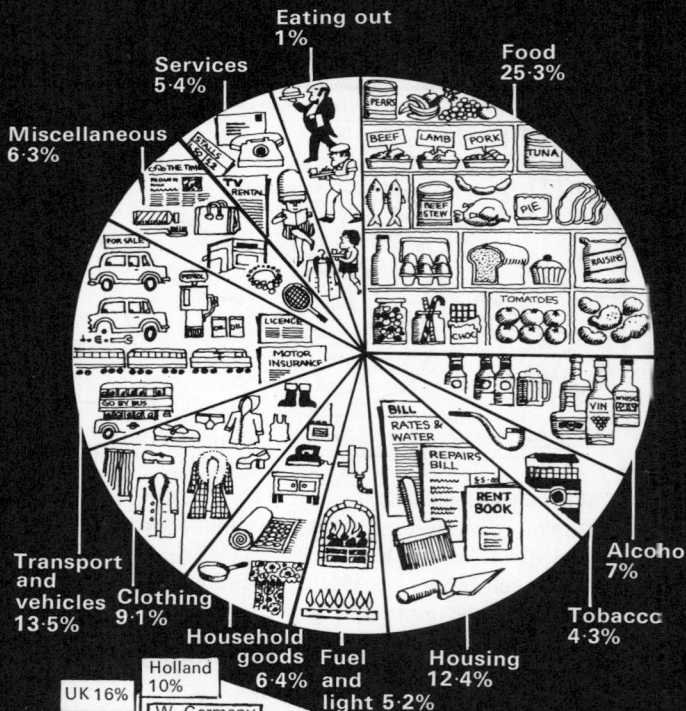

- Canada 11%
- USA 11%
- Brazil 30%
- Chile 793%
- Argentina 24%
- UK 16%
- Holland 10%
- France 13%
- W. Germany 6%
- Italy 19%
- Israel 39%
- USSR 0%
- India 41%
- Japan 32%
- Nigeria 20%
- Zaire 40%
- S. Africa 11%
- Australia 19%

39

A Comprehension
1 Who suffers from inflation?
2 What do we all agree?
3 What do you understand by the term 'bread-winner'?
4 What happens to his pay-packet?
5 What can't the housewife keep up with? Why?
6 What do we call the money that a housewife spends on food, etc. every week?
7 Which people suffer particularly?
8 Who are 'pensioners'?
9 What can't people do when prices are going up all the time?
10 What could the Government do about a) money; b) its own spending; c) taxes; d) wages and prices?
11 What is a hire purchase agreement? What could the Government do about such agreements?
12 What could it do about company profits and interest rates?

B Study the proposals to control inflation and then discuss these questions:
1 Which do you think is the best proposal? Why?
2 Which measures (if any) have been taken in this country to try and control inflation? When? What were or have been the results?
3 For each proposal, answer these questions:
   a) What would this mean for industry?
   b) What would it mean for people on fixed incomes?
   c) What would it mean for the rich?
   d) What would it mean for me (and my family)?

C Are these statements True or False? What's your opinion? Why?
1 'The Government's to blame for inflation—not me!'
2 'The only real answer to inflation and the problems caused by inflation is a change of attitude on the part of the man in the street.'
3 'Inflation will be the downfall of industrialised society.'
4 'Inflation is like sin: every government denounces it and every government practises it.' (Sir Frederick Leith-Ross: 'Observer Sayings of the Week', 30th June, 1957)

D Talking points
1 Discuss some of the main causes of inflation.
2 Suggest ways that the Government in this country could a) cut its own spending; b) raise more taxes.
3 Is hire purchase (or any other form of credit buying) popular in this country? Do you think it is a good or a bad thing? Why?
4 'Like the atomic bomb, inflation is a fact of life. We must learn to live with it.' What do you think?

E This cartoon may be funny because it takes the subject to an extreme. But how many more things won't *you* be able to afford to do if inflation gets any worse?

Owing to Inflation I can't afford to post this letter..

STATISTIC

My life is a curtained window,
A refraction of light in the mirror,
I am a flash in a snow-covered field,
Brilliant in brightness,
Not a torch in the mist
But in clear daylight.
I am the herald before the king
In bright silk, overshadowed
And so forgotten.
I am the unidentified face in the album,
A passport name, a reply in a census,
One more figure in the population statistics,
Dead while I am alive,
Only alive when dead
Until the statistics are changed.

Tom Holt (aged 11)

A Comprehension and Interpretation
1 How does the poet first describe his life? Why, do you think?
2 Why does he describe himself as 'a flash in a snow-covered field' and as 'a torch...in clear daylight'? What have they in common?
3 He feels 'overshadowed' and 'forgotten'. Why, do you think?
4 Which other phrases show us that he feels anonymous in society?
5 What does he mean by 'Dead while I am alive,/Only alive when dead'?
6 Is the poem only about population statistics? What is it about?

B In this modern world you are just a statistic.

a I disagree!
1 Everyone has a personality—expressed in job and hobbies.
2 Relatives, friends and colleagues rely on you as a person.
3 Not just a number (e.g. in a census)— but an individual with an identity—name and address.
4 People have personal characteristics: only machines and robots are referred to by number.

b I agree!
1 Whatever your job/profession—you are dispensable.
2 Just one of millions—most people not even missed when they die.
3 Just a number—in fact a number of numbers—e.g. bank account, passport, telephone, driving licence, etc.
4 Face, habits, dress, personal characteristics —all unimportant in a census, for example.

C What's your opinion? Give reasons.
1 A lot of people think or feel as the poet does, but they can't express themselves. Do you agree?
2 Do you ever feel like the poet? When?
3 If you met the poet, what would you like to say to him/ask him?
4 Does it worry or disturb you that the poem was written by a young boy?

D Talking points
1 Write a list of as many of your own 'numbers' as you can e.g. driving licence, telephone, bank account, insurance policy, flat or house etc. Is the number in each case more important than your name? To whom? Why?
2 How often do we have a census in this country? Why do we have censuses? Are they really necessary? Why/Why not?
3 It has been said that loneliness is one of the greatest problems in cities today. Do you agree? Why/Why not?

E A quotation: 'Keep interested in your own career, however humble; it is a real possession in the changing fortunes of time.... You are a child of the universe, no less than the trees and the stars; you have a right to be here. And whether or not it is clear to you, no doubt the universe is unfolding as it should.'(*Desiderata* Max Ehrmann: found in Old Saint Paul's Church, Baltimore: dated 1692.)

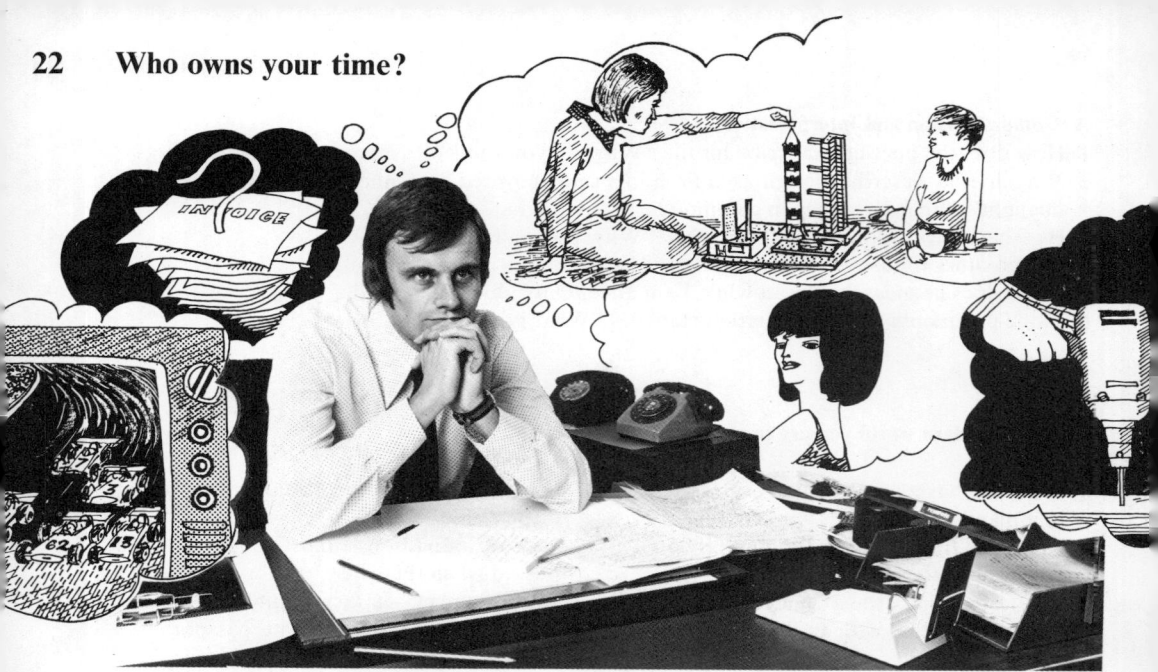

John is 25, works as a clerk in an office, and is married with one child. Paul, a friend of John's, is 30, runs his own business and is single.

JOHN: I'm afraid we shan't be able to come to your party on Friday night, Paul. I've got to work overtime at the office again.

PAUL: What, again? All you seem to do nowadays is work! You didn't come to the concert last week for the same reason. You know what they say, John: 'All work and no play...'

JOHN: I know: '...makes Jack a dull boy.'

PAUL: And I don't know what your wife thinks of it. She must get fed up with your working all the time.

JOHN: She knows that if I want to get on in the job, I've got to work hard now. And we need the money. Sally understands that.

PAUL: Does she? I wonder.

JOHN: OK, so I work overtime now and then...

PAUL: Overtime now and then?! Overwork, you mean. And you know what overwork can lead to—a nervous breakdown, and she's not going to thank you for that.

JOHN: Well, lots of people have no choice in their jobs. Policemen have to work odd hours, for instance. And doctors have to work overtime when there are emergencies. People like that can't choose the hours they work. In that respect, I'm lucky. The firm doesn't own me or my time. I do overtime because I want to.

PAUL: That's what you *think*. You might be fooling yourself.

JOHN: What do you mean?

PAUL: I just wonder what they would think if you said you couldn't work overtime on Friday.

A Comprehension

1 Where were John and his wife going to go on Friday evening?
2 Why can't they go now?
3 What happened last week for the same reason?
4 What saying does Paul quote (and John finish)? What does it mean?
5 How does Paul think Sally feels?
6 What does John say about her?
7 What does Paul wonder?

8 John says he 'works overtime'. Paul says John 'overworks'. What's the difference between the two?
9 What does John say about people like policemen and doctors?
10 What doesn't the firm own, according to John?
11 Why does he do overtime?
12 How is Paul's situation different from John's?

B 'Someone else always owns your time.'

a AGREE

1 Whether married or single, there is little or no time you can call your own.
2 Everyone has commitments: job (perhaps with overtime, work to bring home etc); home life—house, wife, children, car etc.
3 Even time you give to clubs, sport, etc. becomes a permanent commitment—often takes up more time than you originally planned.

b DISAGREE

1 Everyone is born with one great gift— time.
2 You can decide what to do with it.
3 You can rent some of your time to others (in a job) to earn money to live. No need to do more: only fools sell their life and soul to an impersonal company.
4 The wise man chooses his activities carefully and spends x time (and no more) on job, family, leisure, etc.

C What's your opinion? Give reasons.

1 What do you think John's wife thinks of his working overtime?
2 Paul says John 'might be fooling himself'. Do you agree with Paul?
3 What do *you* think the firm would think (and do) if John said he couldn't work overtime?
4 John implies that he's lucky not to be a policeman or a doctor. But is his position really any different from theirs? What do you think?

D Talking points

1 Talk about different professions (e.g. police work, medicine, etc) in which the demands of the job can have disruptive or even disastrous effects on private and family life.
2 'Whatever job you choose, it will own at least 75% of your time.' Discuss.
3 'Even your "free time" is not your own.' True or false. What do you think?

E A quotation: The poet W.H. Davies wrote, in his poem *Leisure*:

> 'What is this life if, full of care,
>   We have no time to stand and stare?'

What do you think he meant by it? How important is this in the 20th century?

FOCUS ON THE ARMS RACE

THE END OF THE WORLD IS AT HAND! —and has been for the past 30+years

FACT! The first atomic bomb was exploded at 5.30 on July 16th, 1945, in the Jornado del Muerto, a desert area in the U.S. Air Force Alamogordo Base in New Mexico. 'Jornado del Muerto' means 'Journey of Death'.

FACT! The world's weapon bill is now more than we spend on education, and is about 9% of the world's total output of goods and services.

FACT! Nearly 20% of the world's scientists are working on projects connected with deterrents (nuclear weapons, inter-continental ballistic missiles, chemical and biological warfare, etc.).

FACT! Many countries in the world now have atomic or nuclear weapons and the facilities for using them. By the year 2000 all the major developing countries in the world will also possess nuclear weapons.

FACT! There have been five major international arms control treaties, as well as the Russian/American Strategic Arms Limitation Talks (SALT). But in spite of these, between 1963 and 1968 the U.S.A. exploded 170 nuclear devices underground and the U.S.S.R., 49. In the world as a whole, the rate of testing has gone up, not down.

WE CAN ALL SEE IT'S CRAZY, SO WHY DOES THE ARMS RACE GO ON?

A Comprehension

1 What happened at 5.30 on July 16th, 1945?
2 What does 'Jornado del Muerto' mean?
3 How does the world's arms bill compare with what we spend on education?
4 What percentage of the world's total output is spent on arms?
5 How many scientists are working on nuclear weapons, etc?
6 What is a 'deterrent'?
7 What do many countries in the world now have?
8 Who will possess nuclear weapons by the year 2000?
9 How many arms control treaties have there been?
10 What does 'SALT' stand for?
11 What did the U.S.A. and the U.S.S.R. do between 1963 and 1968?
12 Has the rate of testing gone down?

B 'The only answer to the fear of nuclear war is total disarmament.'
State the arguments

a FOR

1 Danger of total destruction—only needs one mistake (the wrong button)—world catastrophe!
2 Testing programme adds to world pollution—fall-out—effects on people, animals and plants.
3 Waste of money—so many other things to spend it on.
4 Waste of manpower—esp. scientists— could be working on solution to vital world problems.

b AGAINST

1 Atomic and nuclear weapons are necessary as a deterrent: country X has them—so country Y must have them, too. Question of survival.
2 Vast numbers of people engaged in industry—shutdown of research stations and arms factories—problems.
3 Only answer to the problem—make sure each major power has same number of weapons—maintain real balance.

C Are these statements True or False? What's your opinion? Why?

1 'World peace is an ideal. Total disarmament would not bring it about.'
2 'As long as the major powers continue the arms race, there is no way you can persuade developing countries not to join in.'
3 'Arms limitation talks have a greater chance of success than disarmament talks.'

D Talking points

1 Talk about the other things that money could be spent on instead of arms.
2 What are the other 'world problems' that scientists could be engaged on if they were not working on projects connected with the arms race?
3 Discuss some of the problems that complete disarmament would bring with it e.g. workers employed at present in the arms industry; money spent on arms; land, offices, machinery etc used in the industry, etc.
4 What, in your opinion, is the best reason for stopping the arms race? Why?

E Suggested reading: *On The Beach* by Nevil Shute (Longman Structural Reader Stage 6)

5-MINUTE FORUM

Is this the way to stop accidents?

Situation: Imagine that the Government has just put forword some new proposals to try and solve the problems of overcrowded roads and the steady increase in the number of road accidents.

The first and most controversial proposal is that only people between the ages of 30 and 60 should be allowed to drive.

A group of people have been invited to a TV studio to say what they think of the proposal.

Total drivers killed or seriously injured by age group (Great Britain 1973)

Driving Instructor: It's a bold idea, but a good one, I think. Very young drivers want to drive fast all the time whatever the conditions. And older drivers are often too slow in emergencies.

Company Director: That's a ridiculous generalisation! I'm sixty-five and I drive myself everywhere. You can't stop someone from driving because of his age!

Conservationist: But we do already restrict drivers on the grounds of age! A 15-year-old can't drive in this country. Whatever the arguments, however, I'm in favour of the proposal. The fewer cars there are, the less pollution there'll be.

Travelling Salesman: Well, I think the proposal is mad! Like many people, my job depends on my being able to drive up and down the country. I'm twenty-five, with a wife and two children. I'll have to find a new job!

Police Inspector: Personally, I'm in favour of the idea. Over half the accidents on the roads are caused by drivers under 30 and over 60. Just look at the figures!

Traffic Expert: This proposal will have no effect at all. There will be just as many vehicles on the roads. Firms will employ drivers between 30 and 60 to drive their lorries and vans—and there'll always be someone in every family the right age to drive the family car.

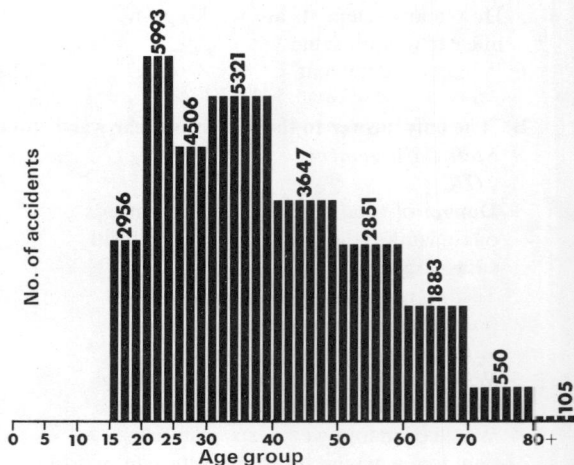

A Comprehension

1 What problems does the Government want to solve?
2 Who will be allowed to drive if the proposal is accepted?
3 What does the driving instructor say about young drivers?
4 In what kinds of situations are old people's reactions slow?
5 How old is the company director?

6 What does he think? Why?
7 Why is the conservationist in favour of the proposal?
8 What does the travelling salesman's job depend on?
9 Why is the police inspector in favour of the idea?
10 What is the traffic expert's opinion? Why does he say that?

B Only people between the ages of 30 and 60 should be allowed to drive.
Summarise the viewpoint of each of the people in the programme:

1 Driving Instructor: bold idea—good one: young drivers—fast all the time: older drivers—slow—emergencies.
2 Company Director: generalisation: 65—drives himself everywhere: age alone not a reason to ban drivers.
3 Conservationist: already restrict driving on the grounds of age: nevertheless—in favour: fewer cars—less pollution.
4 Travelling Salesman: proposal—mad: must be able to drive—job depends on it: 25—wife—2 children: new job.
5 Police Inspector: in favour of proposal: over ½ accidents—caused by under-30's and over-60's. Look at figures.
6 Traffic Expert: Proposal will have no effect: as many vehicles on roads: firms—drivers between 30 and 60: always one person in every family—right age.

And now: Do *you* agree with the proposal that driving should be restricted to the 30–60 age-group? Why/Why not?

C For further discussion

a If you are a driver—
1 How old are you, and how long have you been driving?
2 Have you ever had an accident?
3 If you have, what happened?
4 If not, do you think you will have one day? Why/Why not?
5 What things do other road-users do that annoy you? Why?

b If you are not a driver—
1 Do you want to learn, or are you learning now? Why/Why not?
2 Have there been times when you would like to have been able to drive?
3 How do you usually travel—by bicycle, on foot, etc? Why?
4 Do drivers annoy you at all? Why/Why not?

D Describe how the driving test is conducted in this country. Then make a list of things that you would like to see added to the test: e.g. an intelligence test? a test at night? a thorough medical examination? a test on a motorway? a test in two or three different vehicles? etc. For each proposal you make, give a reason.

E Assignment: Make your own list of proposals which you feel would reduce the number of road-accidents.

'Let's Stop Supersonic Transport Now!'

The arguments
FOR

1 It is important to stop producing supersonic transport (SST) planes now. The disadvantages outweigh the advantages.

2 There is no need for people to travel faster. Already businessmen and politicians who travel a lot are advised to rest before doing business or entering into discussions or important negotiations. Lack of efficiency as a result of crossing time-zones is now a fact.

3 The cost, already millions of pounds, increases every day. The money could be spent better on housing, hospitals, social services, etc.

4 In our present energy crisis, SST planes use far too much fuel.

5 The noise—especially the sonic boom—causes damage to property, people and animals. (The sound waves break windows and even stop hens laying!)

6 Scientists fear the results of pollution. An increase in clouds is possible. There could also be a reduction in the amount of ozone gas in the atmosphere. Both could seriously affect the climate of the earth.

2 The world is already 'smaller' than it was at the beginning of the century. Important that businessmen and politicians can travel to other countries as quickly as possible.

3 The project gives work to thousands —also in many ancillary industries which produce small parts etc.

1 We must go on researching and producing SST planes. Too much has been invested in it (men and money) and too much gained to stop now.

4 The production of SST planes has already proved the possibility of international industrial co-operation.

5 Technological discoveries made during work on SST will be of value in other spheres of life. As with the space programme, this 'spin-off' cannot be ignored.

The arguments
AGAINST

A Comprehension

Look at the arguments for:

1 Why must we stop producing SST planes now?
2 Why are politicians and businessmen already advised to rest?
3 What could the money be spent on?
4 How much fuel do SST planes use?
5 What sort of damage does the sonic boom cause?
6 What do scientists fear? Why?

Look at the arguments against:

1 Why must we go on with SST?
2 What must businessmen and politicians be able to do?
3 How many people are employed in the production of supersonic planes?
4 What do we call industries that produce small parts for a larger project?
5 What has the project proved?
6 What do you understand by 'spin-off'?

B Refer to these notes and state the arguments for and against:

a FOR

1 Important—stop producing SST planes. Disadvantages/advantages.
2 No need—travel faster. Businessmen and politicians—advised rest—lack of efficiency—time-zones.
3 Cost—increases every day: better spent on housing etc.
4 Noise—sonic boom—damage to property, people, animals. Fuel.
5 Scientists—pollution. Increase—clouds. Reduction—ozone in atmosphere. Both—climate.

b AGAINST

1 Must go on—research and production. Too much invested—gained.
2 World—already 'smaller'—even more important—businessmen and politicians—travel quickly.
3 Project—work to thousands—also in ancillary industries.
4 Production of SST planes—international co-operation.
5 Technological discoveries—SST—value—other spheres. e.g. space programme—'spin-off'—ignored.

C Are these statements True or False? What's your opinion? Why?

1 'If we try and stop scientific and technological progress, we shall go back to the Middle Ages.'
2 'SST should be abandoned because it will only benefit a privileged few.'
3 '20th century man is obsessed with speed—with getting from A to B faster than he did yesterday.'
4 'Scientists have no need to worry. A few more jet planes in our atmosphere are not going to cause an ecological catastrophe.'

D Talking Points

1 Talk about some other developments in transport e.g. monorail, hovercraft, electric cars etc. Are any of them being developed in this country?
2 'Airlines can't afford to buy and run SST planes.' 'Airlines can't afford *not* to buy SST planes.' Which statement would you support? Why?

E A proverb: 'More haste, less speed.' What do you think it means? How does it apply to different aspects of twentieth century life?

26   Just a lot of red tape?

Study this form carefully. DON'T FILL IT IN. Mark with an X any information you *would not* like to give to a stranger. (See page 61.)

Full name (Mr/Mrs/Miss)		Address		Tel. No.	
Date of birth		Place of birth		Profession	
Married	Single		Widower		Widow
Height	Weight		Distinguishing features		
Number of dependants		Give names		and ages	
Years at above address as	(a) owner		(b) tenant		(c) with parents
Name of employer		Business address		Business Tel. No.	
Number of years with this employer			Present position		
If self-employed, state occupation, business address and tel.					
Annual income		Bank		Account No.	
If you own your house, please give the exact value					
Do you owe money to anyone?		How much?		To whom?	
Have you lived abroad?		When?		How long?	
Do you intend to live abroad?		Where?		How long?	
Name of doctor		How long has he known you?			
When did you last visit him?		Why?			
Do you smoke?	How much?		Do you drink?		How much?
If married, please give details of husband or wife:					
First names		Age		Occupation	
Name and address of employer			Annual income		

51

A Comprehension

1 Which facts required by the form

a can easily be discovered by a complete stranger?

b are generally known about you by people you don't know very well?

c are usually known about you only by close friends or your family?

2 Which facts required by the form would you say are *very* private?

3 Which are not *very* private?

4 How many X's did you mark? What percentage (approx.) of the total information asked for is that?

5 How many of you put (or would put) an X beside the following: annual income; exact value of your house; when did you last visit your doctor? Why?

B 'There's nothing wrong with forms like this.' State the arguments.

a FOR

1 People don't mind giving information.

2 The information is necessary. Society can't work without it.

3 All the information is basic—not very private.

4 No one can obtain it easily once it is on computer tapes.

b AGAINST

1 People don't like giving information.

2 More questions than necessary.

3 Information not basic—much of it private e.g. health.

4 Information can fall into the wrong hands —be used against people.

5 Evils: blackmail, police state, etc.

C What's your opinion? Give reasons.

1 How much could a stranger learn about you if he read your answers to the questions in this form? What could he deduce? Does this worry you?

2 What do you understand by 'red tape'? Is the form opposite an example of it?

3 What sorts of common things do you have to fill in forms for? Do you object to filling in forms?

4 When did you last fill in a form? Did you answer all the questions?

D Talking points

1 If a 'research worker' stopped you in the street and asked you questions about your private life, would you answer them? Why/Why not?

2 How can information in forms be used (a) in a good way, (b) in a bad way?

3 What happens to the information we provide in forms? What decisions are made on the basis of this information?

4 'Now that we have computers, storing information is not the same as it used to be.' Why isn't it the same? Is this good or bad?

5 'Bits of paper rule our lives.' True or false? Why?

E A quotation: Here are two lines from a poem called *Mending Wall* by the American poet, Robert Frost. What do they mean, and why are they quoted here?

'Before I built a wall, I'd ask to know
What I was walling in or walling out.'

The Little Girl and the Wolf

ONE afternoon a big wolf waited in a dark forest for a little girl to come along carrying a basket of food to her grandmother. Finally a little girl did come along and she was carrying a basket of food. 'Are you carrying that basket to your grandmother?' asked the wolf. The little girl said yes, she was. So the wolf asked her where her grandmother lived and the little girl told him and he disappeared into the wood.

When the little girl opened the door of her grandmother's house she saw that there was somebody in bed with a nightcap and nightgown on. She had approached no nearer than twenty-five feet from the bed when she saw that it was not her grandmother but the wolf, for even in a nightcap a wolf does not look any more like your grandmother than the Metro-Goldwyn lion[1] looks like Calvin Coolidge[2]. So the little girl took an automatic out of her basket and shot the wolf dead.

Moral: It is not so easy to fool little girls nowadays as it used to be.

---

[1] The trade mark of the Metro-Goldwyn film studio.
[2] President of the U.S.A. (1872–1933).

from *The Thurber Carnival*
by James Thurber

A Comprehension
1 Where did the wolf wait?
2 Who was he waiting for?
3 What did he hope she would be doing?
4 What happened finally?
5 What did the wolf ask the girl?
6 What did he ask about the little girl's grandmother?
7 What did the wolf do after this?
8 What did the girl see when she opened the door of her grandmother's house?
9 How far away from the bed was she when she realised it was the wolf?
10 Was it easy to recognise him? Why?
11 What did she do?

B Say what each thinks the other thinks, and why each did what he/she did.
  Attitudes
a The little girl thinks the wolf thinks
1 she—simple-minded—believe him.
2 he can trick her—eat her.
b The wolf thinks the little girl thinks
1 he—kind—won't hurt grandmother.
2 she is safe—wolf won't harm her.

  Behaviour
a Expected: meeting in forest—food—basket—grandmother—bed—nightcap—nightgown.
b Unexpected: took out automatic—shot wolf dead.

C 'It's not so easy to fool little girls nowadays.' What's your opinion?
  AGREE: Children mature more quickly, physically and mentally.
            This is a result of our modern world—TV, newspapers, pop, etc.
            Parents can't protect children from society.
            Schools no longer simply concerned with teaching, reading, writing etc: emphasis on discovering world for yourself.
  DISAGREE: Children always believe what their elders tell them.
            They *seem* to be mature, but they are not.
            All their experience of the world is second-hand (through TV, etc).
            Many dangers in society (e.g. drugs)—children can be fooled.

D Talking points
1 Tell the original 'Little Red Riding Hood' story. How has Thurber changed it? Does it make the story more meaningful for readers today? Why/Why not?
2 Did you enjoy this fable? Why/Why not?
3 What do you think of your best friend? ('I think he's/she's...')
4 What do you think your best friend thinks of you? ('I think my best friend thinks I'm...')
5 What do you think your best friend thinks you think of him/her? ('My best friend thinks I think he's/she's...')
6 'Stories with a moral are not popular any more.' Do you agree?

E Think of a story to illustrate this moral: 'You can fool some of the people some of the time, but you can't fool all of the people all of the time.'

28

FOCUS ON MARRIAGE

'To love and honour ...in sickness and in health...for richer, for poorer...for better, for worse... till death us do part.'

These are part of the vows made by the man and the woman in an English marriage ceremony. But how many young people about to get married think about what they mean?

John Lucas and Mary Holmes, both 24, have decided to get married soon. But the traditional vows aren't enough for them. They want a legal contract which will define their respective obligations and expectations when they are married. By talking about their marriage, John and Mary have had to examine why they want to marry and what they expect of each other. This is the document which they now want a solicitor to put into a legal contract for each of them to sign:

WE WANT TO DECLARE THAT:

1. We intend to marry each other in the near future.
2. We want to set out the conditions for our future marriage.
3. The conditions in the contract will refer to our respective marital rights, and our obligations to each other and any children we may have.

THE CONDITIONS WE WANT TO AGREE TO AND SIGN ARE

1. Mary will keep her own surname after we are married.
2. We shall continue our separate careers and help each other in them.
3. We shall decide together where to live.
4. We shall respect each other's private property, and regard anything bought jointly after we are married as joint property.
5. We shall have separate bank accounts, but both contribute (depending on our incomes) to the payment of bills for food, the house etc.
6. We shall both share in the management of the home (e.g. cleaning).
7. We shall have equal responsibility in bringing up any children and providing them with food, clothes, shelter and education etc. until they are 18.
8. We want to be able to revise this contract at any time if either of us is dissatisfied.
9. Throughout our marriage we intend to a) talk about how it is going; b) tell each other where we are; c) spend most of our leisure time together.
10. If we have a disagreement which we cannot resolve, then we agree to go to a third person e.g. a marriage guidance counsellor, priest, etc.

A Comprehension

1 What have John and Mary decided?
2 What do they think about traditional marriage rows?
3 What do they want? What will it do?
4 What have they had to examine?
5 What three things do they want to declare?
6 What name will Mary have when they are married?
7 Is Mary going to stop work? Why?
8 Who will decide where they live?
9 What will happen to their own property when they marry?
10 What sort of bank accounts will they have?
11 How will they pay bills?
12 How will responsibility for bringing up children be shared?
13 What else do they intend to do?

B 'Every married couple should make a legal contract.' Do you agree?

a YES, because
1 it makes them look at the proposed relationship realistically, not through a 'love-haze'.
2 they try and foresee difficulties.
3 it will ensure *joint* decisions and responsibility e.g. when and where to marry; where to live; etc.
4 it clarifies the expectations of both husband and wife.

b NO, because
1 a good marriage is based on love: can't write love into a legal document; vows— an unwritten contract.
2 traditional vows say everything.
3 if a couple think they'll have second thoughts, they shouldn't get married.
4 both know what to expect already: they *want* to get married.

C Are these statements True or False? What's your opinion? Why?

1 'Contracts of this sort can only lead to a further deterioration in the idea of marriage and its purpose.'
2 'If a woman wants to follow a career, she shouldn't get married and have children.'
3 'Marriage is not an end but a beginning.'
4 'A good arranged marriage is likely to be far more successful than any marriage for love'.

D Talking points

1 Describe a traditional marriage ceremony in this country.
2 Talk about different 20th century experiments in marriage e.g. contract marriages (as here), community living, and so on.
3 Is the traditional concept of marriage 'for better, for worse. . . till death us do part' realistic in the 20th century? Why/Why not?
4 Who gets the best deal in a marriage in this country—the man or the woman? Why do you say that? Is it right? Why/Why not?

E A quotation: 'Inside every marriage there are two marriages: "his" and "hers".' (from *The Future of Marriage* by Jessie Bernard)

Viewpoint

Live and let live!

Sir,

I am writing to protest at the way scientists use animals for cruel experiments. Scientists say that these experiments are conducted 'for the benefit of mankind'. But there is *no argument* which can justify the unnecessary suffering inflicted on animals. And further, scientists know very well that most of their experiments on animals can benefit no one. Indeed, some experiments (like grafting a second head onto a living creature) are so grotesque that they diminish the dignity of man.

Animals are abused and exploited, yet—without realising it—they can only depend on us for protection. If we don't protect them, who will? If you saw a man publicly beating a dog, you would be shocked and angry. But a scientist can perform all kinds of unspeakable horrors in the privacy of his laboratory in the name of 'research'.

It's time animals were allowed to enjoy the gift of life as much as we are and they will only do so when 'scientific experiments' are banned for ever.

Yours etc.,

John Walton

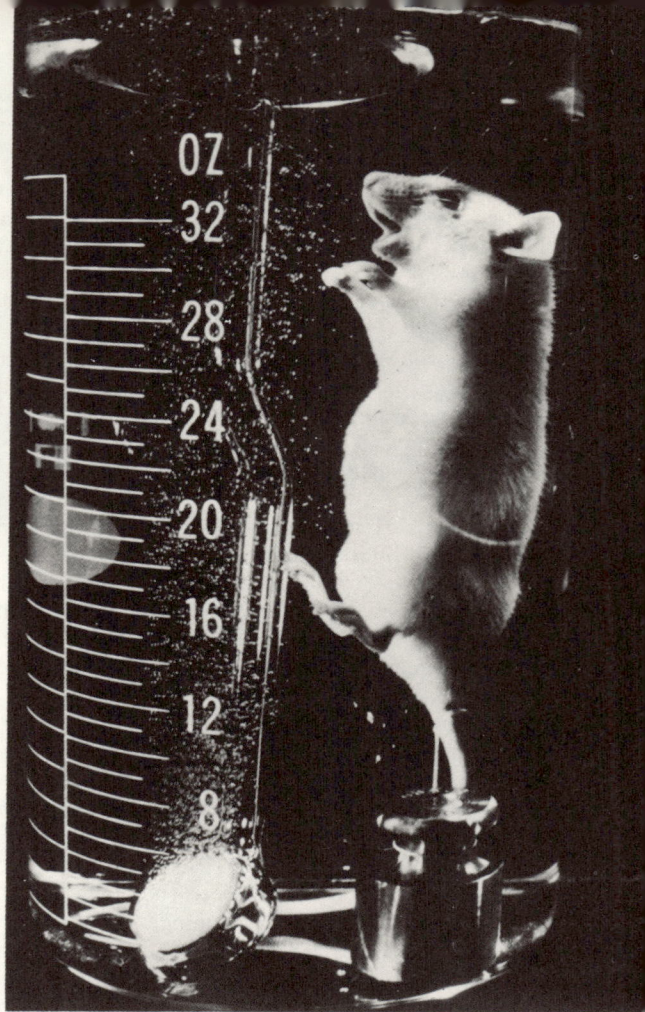

A mouse equipped to breathe underwate a laboratory experimen

John Walton

LIVING TARGETS

Sheep used in bullet tests

A Comprehension

1 What is John Walton protesting about?

2 How do scientists defend these experiments?

3 According to Mr Walton, what is there no argument for?

4 What example does he give of a 'grotesque' experiment?

5 What do such experiments do to man?

6 Why must we protect animals?

7 Who will protect them if we don't?

8 How would most of us feel if we saw a man publicly beating a dog?

9 What can a scientist do in the name of 'research'? Where?

10 What does Mr Walton want animals to be able to do?

11 When will that be, according to him?

B 'Scientific experiments on live animals should be banned.'

a I agree

1 Animals are defenceless: hurt in many experiments.

2 Don't have to use animals—could use human volunteers (or find other methods). Animals can't describe symptoms—humans can.

3 Might be some justification for trying out medicine—but *no* argument for operations, pure research, etc.

b I disagree

1 New areas of medicine and surgery—experiments necessary: must be safe for humans—so must use live animals.

2 The life of just one animal might save the lives of thousands of humans.

3 Scientists make every effort to make sure animals do not suffer: these scientists are not sadists!

4 Most experiments really are for the benefit of mankind'.

C What's your opinion? Give reasons.

1 Do you agree with the writer of the letter?

2 If you do, then perhaps you believe that new medicines, for example, should be tried out on human beings. Would you volunteer or allow a member of your family to volunteer for such experiments?

3 If you don't agree with the writer, would you allow scientists to perform experiments on your pets (cat, dog, bird etc)?

D Talking points

1 Talk about the many different ways in which we use, abuse or exploit animals. Talk about cattle, dolphins, elephants, horses, dogs, rats, mice, monkeys, pigeons and others. Can one defend a distinction between pets, domestic animals and animals for 'research'?

2 One of the most controversial medical events this century has been the birth of 'thalidomide' babies. Perhaps if the drug (given to mothers) had been *fully* tried out on animals, disaster would have been averted. What do you think?

E A problem: A close relative of yours is seriously ill. A cure has been found, but it has not yet been proved safe by experiment. The doctors want to try it out on your relative. It's the only hope. What would you say? Why?

30   Over whose dead body?

MARGARET: **Governments give in to hijackers' demands too easily. A hijacker has only got to threaten to blow up a plane or commit some outrage, and a government gives in to his demands.**

VALERIE: **Naturally. It's the lesser of two evils. Which government could put innocent lives at risk just to see if terrorists will really do what they threaten to do? Terrorists have proved often enough that they really mean business.**

MARGARET: **Yes, but if a government doesn't hold out against this kind of blackmail, we will *always* have terrorists. Governments are afraid to punish these people and are only too glad to let them go free. Start executing terrorists automatically wherever they land, and terrorism will stop.**

VALERIE: **And what about all the innocent lives that will be lost in the process? Terrorism is based on the simple idea of threatening the innocent to achieve its ends.**

MARGARET: **You can't get rid of evil without being prepared to face the consequences of evil.**

VALERIE: **So long as you aren't one of the victims!**

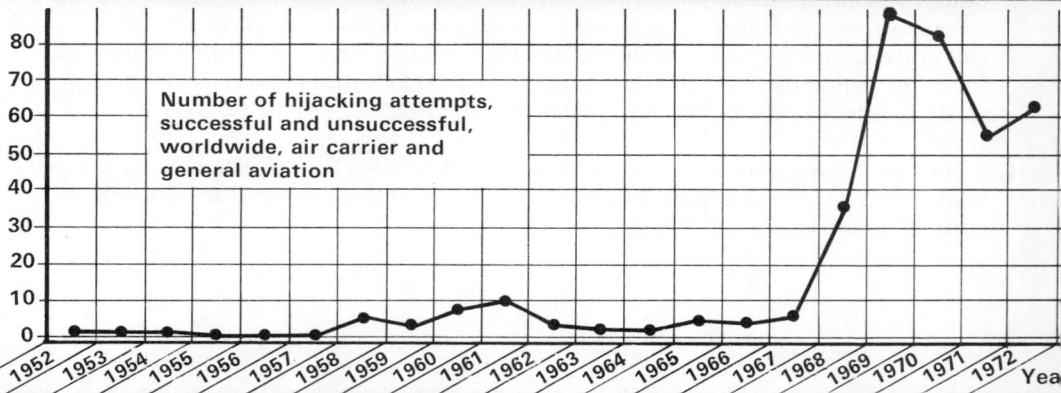

Number of hijacking attempts, successful and unsuccessful, worldwide, air carrier and general aviation

A Comprehension

1 According to Margaret, what do governments do too easily?

2 What must a hijacker do to make a government give in to his demands?

3 Valerie says: 'It's the lesser of two evils.' Which 'two evils' is she talking about?

4 How have terrorists proved that they 'mean business'?

5 According to Margaret, 'we will *always* have terrorists'. If what?

6 What are governments afraid to do?—and 'only too glad' to do?

7 What is Margaret's solution to the problem?

8 Who is Valerie concerned about?

9 She says terrorism is based on a simple idea. What simple idea?

10 What do you think Margaret means by 'the consequences of evil'?

11 What does Valerie's last comment mean?

B Two points of view

a State Margaret's point of view

1 Whenever there is a threat, or a plane is burnt or blown up—governments give in to hijackers.

2 Governments must make a stand against this sort of blackmail.

3 Solution: be firm—arrest and execute hijackers wherever they land. (Innocent people might be killed or injured—a risk that must be taken. Could stop hijacking once and for all.)

b State Valerie's point of view

1 Governments don't give in *too* easily. Their concern—innocent passengers.

2 Governments know—hijackers not usually bluffing. They've proved often—they mean business.

3 Solution: international agreement on stricter security checks. Make it impossible for would-be hijackers to take guns and other weapons on to planes.

C What's your opinion?

1 Who do you agree with, Margaret or Valerie? Why?

2 If no damage is done and no one is killed or injured, do you think hijackers should be punished? If so, how? If not, why not?

3 Why do you think there has been a steady increase in hijacking over the past few years?

D Talking points

1 Discuss ways to stop hijacking.

2 Has there been a hijacking recently? Where? When? What did the hijackers want and what did they do? What did the authorities do? What was the outcome? What is your opinion of the actions of (a) the hijackers; and (b) the authorities? Would you have done the same as the authorities? Why/Why not? What else would you have done?

E From whose point of view are terrorists and hijackers: a) heroes, b) cowards, c) madmen, d) fanatics?

Notes

Lesson 26 (page 51)

The questions you have studied on the form on page 51 are just a few of the questions to which many of us give answers when we see the following forms:

an application for life insurance

an application for property insurance

an application for a credit card

a national census form

an application for credit facilities at a large store

a consumer market survey

Can you think of any more that you might have filled in during the past year?

Some useful phrases

A Making a point/Stating an argument

1 In my opinion, . . .
2 Personally, I think . . .
3 I believe (that) . . .
4 The point is this: . . .
5 If you ask me, I think . . .
6 I'd like to say this: . . .
7 As far as I'm concerned, . . .

C Clarifying

1 What I said/meant was: . . .
2 I did *not* say . . . . What I *did* say
   was . . .
3 I think you (must have) misunderstood
   me/what I said.
4 Let me repeat/rephrase what I said.
5 I'm not saying that. What I *am* saying
   is (that) . . .
6 Yes, but don't forget I was only
   referring to . . .

E Disagreeing with an argument

1 (I'm afraid) I disagree.
2 On the other hand, of course, . . .
3 That's not (entirely) true, . . .
4 I can't possibly agree with/accept that.
5 I hate to disagree with you, but . . .
6 Yes/All right, but don't you think . . .

G Asking for an opinion

1 Well? What do *you* think?
2 Do/Don't you agree?
3 What's your view (then)?
4 How do you see it (then)?
5 Let's have your opinion.

B Challenging an argument

1 That can't be (true/right).
2 But what about . . . ? What's your answer
   to that?
3 Do you mean to tell me that . . . ?
4 Are you seriously suggesting that . . . ?
5 If you don't . . . , then you should say what
   you mean.

D Agreeing with an argument

1 Quite.
2 Exactly.
3 That's (very) true.
4 So (do) I. Neither/Nor (do) I.
5 I entirely agree.
6 I agree with you entirely.
7 You're absolutely right.
8 That's a good point.
9 I couldn't agree with you more.
10 That's just what I think.

F Interrupting an argument

1 Excuse me, did you say/do you mean
   (that) . . .
2 Before you make your next point . . .
3 So what you're saying is (that) . . .
4 Come to the point! What you really think
   is (that) . . .

H Summarising a discussion

1 Then we agree.
2 (Basically), we're in agreement.
3 (I think) we'd better agree to differ.

Also by LG Alexander

Language Practice Books:
Sixty Steps to Précis
Poetry and Prose Appreciation for Overseas
  Students
Essay and Letter-writing
A First Book in Comprehension, Précis and
  Composition
Question and Answer: Graded Aural/Oral
  Exercises
Reading and Writing English
Guided Composition in English Language
  Teaching
In Other Words

The Carters of Greenwood (Cineloops):
Teacher's Handbook
Elementary Workbook
Intermediate Workbook

Look, Listen and Learn:
Pupils' Books 1–4
Teacher's Books 1–4
Workbooks-Link Readers

New Concept English:
First Things First
Practice and Progress
Developing Skills
Fluency in English
Mainline Progress A & B
Mainline Skills A & B
Students' Books and Teacher's Books

Target 1–3
Pupils' and Teacher's Books
  with J Tadman and RH Kingsbury

Longman Structural Readers, Stage 1:
Detectives from Scotland Yard
Car Thieves
Mr Punch

Longman Structural Readers, Stage 2:
April Fools' Day
Worth a Fortune
Professor Boffin's Umbrella
K's First Case

Longman Structural Readers, Stage 3:
Operation Mastermind
Good morning, Mexico!
Dangerous Game
Clint Magee

Longman Integrated Comprehension
  and Composition Series:
    General Editor
Tell Us a Story
Mainline
English Grammatical Structure
Uniform with this Volume:
  For and Against:
    An Oral Practice Book for Advanced
    Students of English

  Make your point
  30 Discussion Topics for Students at
    Secondary Level